# Timeshare Vacations
# For Dummies®, 1st Edition

Cheat Sheet

## Packing for a Timeshare

D1073294

Your home away from home won't be com
little necessities that you take for granted

Many resorts offer small starter packages of kitchen and bathroom supplies,
many resorts also offer convenience stores that sell basic supplies and food.
Expect to pay a little more for convenience-store items, as opposed to buying
in bulk at your local chain or home center. Towels, linens, serving wear (plates,
glasses, cutlery), cooking pots and pans, small appliances, TV/VCR/DVD, CD player,
microwave, washer/dryer, dishwasher, telephones, hair dryers, dataports, alarm
clocks, and irons and ironing boards are supplied in most timeshare resort units.
But always find out exactly what's offered (and what you need to bring with you)
before you go. Of course, in addition to the suggestions in the following list, you
may want to include other essential items that you can't live without for a week.

- **Your RCI or II membership card and your confirmation from RCI or II:** You
  need to present your membership card when you check in, and it's always
  smart to have your confirmation on hand in the (unlikely) event that your
  reservation is lost.

- **Kitchen/laundry supplies:** Laundry detergent, fabric softener, dishwashing
  liquid, dishwasher detergent, kitchen sponge or dishwashing brush, general
  cleaning solutions, coffee filters and coffee, paper towels, and oven mitt.

- **Cooking supplies:** Salt, pepper, and any other spices you expect to use;
  ketchup, mustard, mayonnaise, and any condiments you expect to use;
  aluminum foil, plastic baggies, garbage bags; plastic containers; and flour,
  sugar, and basic nonperishable foodstuffs you plan to cook with (pasta and
  rice, canned soups, canned tuna, cooking oils, vinegar, and the like).

- **Bathroom supplies:** Toilet paper, tissues, soap, and shampoo.

- **Paper goods:** Paper plates, napkins, and cutlery for those days you don't
  want to wash dishes.

- **Prescription medicines and over-the-counter medicines:** First-aid kit,
  aspirin, Q-tips, band-aids, antibacterial cream, and sunscreen.

- **Entertainment:** Music CDs or tapes and/or videotapes, DVDs, books, magazines, card games, tennis rackets, golf clubs, swimsuits, and other sports
  equipment.

- **Miscellaneous:** Candles/candle holders, light bulbs, corkscrew, cocktail
  napkins, stamps, scissors, small sewing kit, good paring knife, umbrella,
  beach towels, and a cooler.

# Florida Timeshare

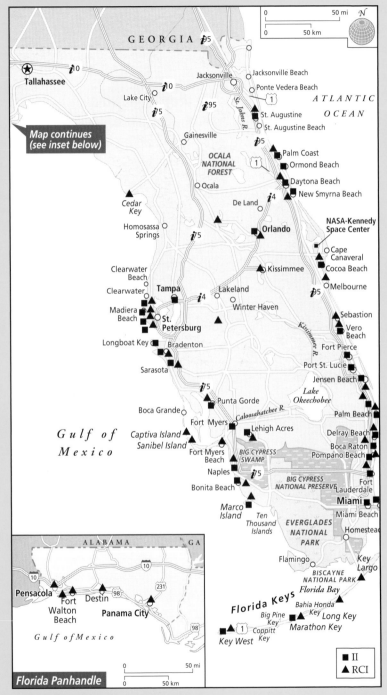

0    50 mi
0    50 km
N

GEORGIA

Tallahassee

Jacksonville
Jacksonville Beach
Ponte Vedera Beach

Lake City

ATLANTIC
OCEAN

St. Augustine
St. Augustine Beach

Gainesville

Map continues
(see inset below)

OCALA
NATIONAL
FOREST

Palm Coast
Ormond Beach

Ocala

Daytona Beach
New Smyrna Beach

Cedar
Key

De Land

Homosassa
Springs

Orlando

NASA-Kennedy
Space Center

Clearwater
Beach

Kissimmee

Cape
Canaveral
Cocoa Beach
Melbourne

Clearwater

Tampa

Lakeland

Madiera
Beach

St.
Petersburg

Winter Haven

Sebastion

Vero
Beach

Longboat Key

Bradenton

Fort Pierce

Sarasota

Punta Gorde

Lake
Okeechobee

Port St. Lucie

Jensen Beach

Boca Grande

Fort Myers

Caloosahatchee R.

Palm Beach

Gulf of
Mexico

Captiva Island
Sanibel Island

Lehigh Acres

Delray Beach

Fort Myers
Beach

BIG CYPRESS
SWAMP

Boca Raton
Pompano Beach

Naples

BIG CYPRESS
NATIONAL PRESERVE

Fort
Lauderdale

Bonita Beach

Miami

Marco
Island

Ten
Thousand
Islands

EVERGLADES
NATIONAL
PARK

Miami Beach

Homestead

Flamingo

BISCAYNE
NATIONAL PARK

Key
Largo

Florida Bay

Florida Keys

Bahia Honda
Big Pine
Key

Key
Long Key
Marathon Key

Key West

Coppitt
Key

ALABAMA

GA

Pensacola

Fort
Walton
Beach

Destin

Panama City

Gulf of Mexico

Florida Panhandle

0    50 mi
0    50 km

■ II
▲ RCI

# FOR DUMMIES®

## The fun and easy way™ to travel!

## U.S.A.

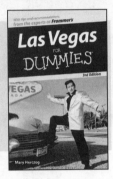

**Also available:**

Alaska For Dummies
Arizona For Dummies
Boston For Dummies
California For Dummies
Chicago For Dummies
Colorado & the Rockies For Dummies
Florida For Dummies
Los Angeles & Disneyland For Dummies
Maui For Dummies
National Parks of the American West For Dummies

New Orleans For Dummies
New York City For Dummies
San Francisco For Dummies
Seattle & the Olympic Peninsula For Dummies
Washington, D.C. For Dummies
RV Vacations For Dummies
Walt Disney World & Orlando For Dummies

## EUROPE

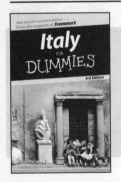

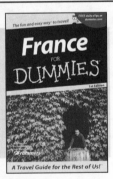

**Also available:**

England For Dummies
Europe For Dummies
Germany For Dummies
Ireland For Dummies
London For Dummies

Paris For Dummies
Scotland For Dummies
Spain For Dummies

## OTHER DESTINATIONS

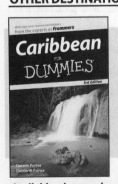

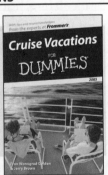

**Also available:**

Bahamas For Dummies
Cancun & the Yucatan For Dummies
Costa Rica For Dummies
Mexico's Beach Resorts For Dummies
Montreal & Quebec City For Dummies
Vancouver & Victoria For Dummies

**Available wherever books are sold.**
**Go to www.dummies.com or call 1-877-762-2974 to order direct.**

# Timeshare Vacations
## FOR
# DUMMIES®
## 1ST EDITION

### by Lisa Ann Schreier

WILEY

Wiley Publishing, Inc.

**Timeshare Vacations For Dummies, 1st Edition**

Published by
**Wiley Publishing, Inc.**
111 River St.
Hoboken, NJ 07030-5774
www.wiley.com

For general information on our other products and services, please contact our Customer Care Department within the U.S. at 800-762-2974, outside the U.S. at 317-572-3993, or fax 317-572-4002.

For technical support, please visit www.wiley.com/techsupport.

Wiley also publishes its books in a variety of electronic formats. Some content that appears in print may not be available in electronic books.

Library of Congress Control Number: 2005923789

ISBN-13: 978-0-7645-8442-8

ISBN-10: 0-7645-8442-1

Manufactured in the United States of America

10  9  8  7  6  5  4  3  2  1

1B/SS/QW/QV/IN

WILEY

# About the Author

**Lisa Ann Schreier** is the founder of Timeshare Insights, an independent and unbiased organization dedicated to guiding consumers through the often mysterious and sometimes tedious world of timeshare. Before moving to the Orlando, Florida, area in 1997, she worked in the advertising and media industry in Chicago, becoming a media buyer for major clients. She formed GRQ Enterprises, an advertising and consulting business providing one-stop marketing expertise for clients.

Since moving to central Florida, she has worked for several timeshare resorts in the Orlando area, as a salesperson, a sales manager, and a trainer. Seeing firsthand the good, the bad, and the ugly in the industry, she first became a contributing columnist to *The Timeshare Beat,* the industry's most widely read publication, where she blended her advertising expertise with her timeshare experience. In 2003, she formed Timeshare Insights, where her focus has been on educating potential and current timeshare owners, believing that an educated consumer can bring about necessary changes to the industry.

Ms. Schreier has been featured on WOR-AM in New York City, the *Chicago Tribune,* the *Los Angeles Times,* the *Baltimore Sun, Hiatus Magazine,* and both WLS-TV and WGN-TV in Chicago. She is a frequent guest speaker at timeshare owners' groups, consumer travel shows, and timeshare management university classes. She is also the author of *Surviving a Timeshare Presentation . . . Confessions from the Sales Table* (Oct. 2004).

You can contact Lisa at www.timeshareinsights.com, or through her agent, Ibach and Associates, at www.ibach sportspr.com.

# Author's Acknowledgments

Thanks to my immediate and extended family and a special "thank you" to those family members who stood by me, encouraged me, and supported me through this project and everything else.

Thanks to my friends, although most of them were mildly bemused by the whole process.

Thanks to my publicist, Bob Ibach, who continually encourages me to strive for the best.

Many thanks to everyone at Wiley: Mike Spring for seeing the need for this book; Kelly Regan for holding my hand through the initial stages; Amy Lyons for being there in the beginning; Lindsay, Ensley, Heather, and April for getting the word out and being so receptive to my media and publicity ideas; and especially Alexis Lipsitz Flippin for taking my sometimes random notes, scribbles, and innumerable e-mails and making a wonderful book out of them. Thanks, too, to Tere Stouffer for her expert Dummies touch and eternal optimism.

Although I contacted, interviewed, and attempted to interview as many people within the industry as possible in order to present the clearest and most independent outlook on timeshare, there are a few people that deserve to be singled out for going above and beyond the call of duty:

David Jimenez of RCI and Christine Boesch of II for providing me with all the information I asked for and helping me learn a great deal about timeshare in the process.

Gregory Coots of Disney Vacation Club who was especially generous with his time and extraordinarily open with the DVC materials and information.

Richard L. Ragatz, PhD, of Ragatz Associates who provided me with many of the research findings.

Antoine Dagot, K. Robert Kreiger, Dennis DeLorenzo, and Elena Norman of Hilton Grand Vacations Club for their time and their candidness.

Jean Kilani of the Berkeley Group for his support and his many thought-provoking discussions with me.

Edward F. Kinney of Marriott Vacation Club International who answered most of my e-mails in record time.

As a last note, both RCI and II were very open with me as I wrote this book, and both shared with me exactly how their resorts are rated.

Thanks, also, to the timeshare owners who shared their experiences with me for the book.

Thanks to Barbara Corcoran for writing me an e-mail that allowed me to take a chance, expand my horizons, and proceed with confidence.

Thanks to Julian, my helpful and always faithful typist.

I could not have written this book and achieved so much without all those people in the timeshare industry who gave me grief, laughed at me, and continually tried to discourage me from doing anything outside the box. With that much resistance, I figured that the book *had* to be written. And it was.

## Publisher's Acknowledgments

We're proud of this book; please send us your comments through our Dummies online registration form located at www.dummies.com/register/.

Some of the people who helped bring this book to market include the following:

### Editorial

**Editors:** Tere Stouffer, Alexis Lipsitz Flippin

**Cartographer:** Roberta Stockwell

**Editorial Manager:** Michelle Hacker

**Editorial Supervisor:** Michelle Hacker

**Editorial Assistant:** Melissa Bennett

**Senior Photo Editor:** Richard Fox

**Cover Photos:** © Michael Melford/ Getty Images; © Neil Emmerson/ Robert Harding World Imagery/ Getty Images

**Cartoons:** Rich Tennant (www.the5thwave.com)

### Composition Services

**Project Coordinator:** Adrienne Martinez

**Layout and Graphics:** Carl Byers, Andrea Dahl, Lynsey Osborn, Melanee Prendergast, Heather Ryan

**Proofreaders:** Leeann Harney, Jessica Kramer, Dwight Ramsey, TECHBOOKS Production Services

**Indexer:** TECHBOOKS Production Services

---

### Publishing and Editorial for Consumer Dummies

**Diane Graves Steele,** Vice President and Publisher, Consumer Dummies

**Joyce Pepple,** Acquisitions Director, Consumer Dummies

**Kristin A. Cocks,** Product Development Director, Consumer Dummies

**Michael Spring,** Vice President and Publisher, Travel

**Kelly Regan,** Editorial Director, Travel

### Publishing for Technology Dummies

**Andy Cummings,** Vice President and Publisher, Dummies Technology/ General User

### Composition Services

**Gerry Fahey,** Vice President of Production Services

**Debbie Stailey,** Director of Composition Services

# Contents at a Glance

# Maps at a Glance

# Table of Contents

# Introduction

*I*magine a man in a polyester leisure suit, sporting a white belt, white shoes, and a big gold chain; smelling of cheap cologne; and flashing a gleaming gold-toothed smile. Imagine the scene as he sweeps his beefy hand over a weed-choked expanse of undeveloped land that smells faintly of peat bogs, and then points proudly to a drawing of a megaluxe condo. Imagine him forcing a pen into some poor unsuspecting consumer's hand as the deal is sealed.

When you imagine this scene, does it say "timeshare" to you? Exaggerated as it may be, it had some semblance to the truth not so long ago. Unfortunately, as good as the product often was, timeshare developed a snake-oil-salesman reputation over the years for its aggressive sales techniques, bait-and-switch schemes, and sleazy profiteers.

The good news is that today timeshare has cleaned up its act considerably and in large part is a respectable and desirable way to increase your vacation and lifestyle quality for years to come. But I still feel there's room for improvement.

Many people ask me, "Do you make money selling timeshare?" The answer is yes. Quite frankly, if I'd never sold timeshare, I wouldn't be in a position to inform consumers about the pros and cons of buying timeshare. My experiences in selling timeshare have allowed me to see where the timeshare industry has failed consumers and failed itself. But I also wouldn't be in the timeshare business if I didn't believe that the product itself — in its many new and wonderful incarnations, whether a simple two-bedroom unit, a bunk on a yacht, a perch in a treehouse, a room in a castle — is quite often superlative and worth every penny.

My problem is not with the product; it's with how timeshare is sold and marketed. I believe that the high-pressure hard sell should be a thing of the past. I always maintain that I never try to sell someone timeshare; I prefer to *let* a person buy — or not buy — as the case may be.

I wrote this book because of what I see as the lack of solid, reliable, no-nonsense information available to consumers interested in buying timeshare. I wrote it to clear up some misconceptions, to help you understand what you're buying, and to steer you clear of buying if that's just not the right choice for you.

This book is neither pro-timeshare nor anti-timeshare. It's just the facts, ma'am, with a sprinkling of my own unvarnished, insider's opinion. Read it, use it, and bring it with you when you view timeshare. Bring it with you when you go to a timeshare sales presentation. Bring it with you so that you know that whatever decision you make, it will be the right decision for you.

# About This Book

This book offers an in-depth look at the timeshare industry, including how to buy timeshare, how to use and exchange timeshare, and how to sell timeshare, even an international one.

If you plan to attend a timeshare presentation, I strongly encourage you to read this book before you go, and by all means, bring it with you for the presentation. It'll help keep the salespeople on their toes and keep the sales presentation from veering off into hard-sell, high-pressure tactics.

# Conventions Used in This Book

*Timeshare Vacations For Dummies,* 1st Edition, is, first and foremost, a reference guide, and as such provides helpful, easy-to-follow conventions. For example, any new terms are italicized, Web addresses are shown in a special font (`like this`), and icons draw your attention to particularly useful text. In addition, both the singular and plural uses of the word "timeshare" are employed throughout the book.

# What You're Not to Read

This book is not meant to be a chronological read; you can skip around to the stuff you're really interested in and get all the information you need. Skip the sidebars, too, if you want — but I'll bet if you glance at a couple, you'll find yourself devouring the rest.

# Foolish Assumptions

This book is written with you, the average vacationer, in mind. (By *average,* I mean someone who likes to go on vacation.) You'll find this book useful if you already own timeshare, if you've never heard of timeshare, or if you fall somewhere in-between.

In this book, I make some of the following assumptions about you and what your needs may be:

- ✔ You've heard about timeshare but never really bothered to investigate whether it was for you.

- ✔ You've suffered through one or more tedious timeshare presentations (called *pitches*), only to come out more confused than when you went in.

✔ You've thought about purchasing a timeshare, but didn't know where to go for unbiased, independent information before making a purchase.

✔ You've already purchased a timeshare and want to find out more about the product and see what's new in the industry.

✔ You're in the timeshare industry and want to help make the industry better by helping to educate the consumer.

# How This Book Is Organized

*Timeshare Vacations For Dummies,* 1st Edition, is organized into five parts. The following sections describe the five parts and an overview of what they contain.

## Part 1: Understanding Timeshare

This part gives you a general definition of what timeshare is, the basic economics of timeshare, information on the types of timeshares out there for purchase, most frequently asked questions about timeshare, and top consumer issues.

## Part II: Buying Timeshare

Part II addresses the marketing of timeshares, those infamous timeshare sales presentations, financing timeshare, buying resale and international timeshare, the top questions you want ask when buying timeshare, and the biggest secrets about timeshares that developers and the marketing companies don't want you to know.

## Part III: Discovering a World of Timeshare

This part addresses the locations of timeshare around the world, describes the different brands and big names in the timeshare business, and discusses *exchanging* — that is, playing the trading game.

## Part IV: Using Your Timeshare

This part includes pertinent information on settling in at your home resort, and how to rent, sell, or will your timeshare. You also discover the popular new variations on timeshare, including fractionals, condo hotels, vacation clubs, and urban interval ownership.

## Part V: The Part of Tens

In this section, I discuss timeshare sales pitches you want to run from, some unusual timeshares you may not have thought of as timeshare, and important timeshare issues every consumer should know.

## *Appendixes*

Appendix A (Quick Concierge) provides contact information for the largest timeshare exchange companies and brand resorts. It's also where you get information on who to contact if you have legal issues regarding timeshare. Appendix B offers you a timeshare glossary, so that you can go head to head with timeshare gurus and hold your own. Appendix C shows the locations of timeshare resorts around the world.

# *Icons Used in This Book*

Icons — little pictures in the margins — are meant to draw your attention to especially useful text. Explanations of what each icon means follow.

Watch for this icon to help you identify annoying or potentially dangerous situations, such as rip-offs, the proverbial if-it-sounds-too-good-to-be-true-it-is situations, and other deceptions to avoid.

This icon points out useful advice on timeshare, including ways to save time and avoid headaches.

This icon alerts you to important things and facts and figures to keep in mind.

This icon alerts you to money-saving timeshare tips.

This icon is used whenever I hear from a timeshare owner who has been generous enough to offer advice on a specific aspect of timeshare.

# *Where to Go from Here*

Any way you look at it, timeshare is a compelling concept and a fast-growing phenomenon. In this book, you'll find out which destinations are the best for families (Chapter 11), where the brand names have set up shop (Chapter 13), and how to make the best of a timeshare presentation (Chapter 6). *Timeshare Vacations For Dummies,* 1st Edition, is meant to be fun to read and informative throughout, so I say jump right in anywhere.

As you peruse this book, check out two special sidebars. The ones marked with the Timeshare Talk icon offer good advice from actual timeshare owners. Those titled "Snapshot: [Destination]" provide practical information and personal thoughts on particular timeshare locations, such as Orlando, Las Vegas, and even Fiji.

# Part I

# Understanding Timeshare

**The 5th Wave**                    By Rich Tennant

# In this part . . .

Timeshare is a young concept, having been invented by entrepreneurs looking for creative ways to resell condominiums. I discuss the basic principles of timeshare and provide lists of the best timeshare resorts, the hottest destinations, the best reasons to buy a timeshare — and the best reasons *not* to buy a timeshare.

# Chapter 1

# Best of Timeshare Vacations

*In This Chapter*

▶ Discovering the best reasons to buy timeshare — and the best reasons not to
▶ Choosing the best resorts
▶ Finding the hottest locations
▶ Uncovering the up-and-coming destinations
▶ Finding the best-value destinations
▶ Exploring the top family-friendly destinations
▶ Getting wise to the top destinations for retirees

*W*ith more than 5,700 timeshare resorts around the world, and some 100 new resorts added each year, the timeshare industry continues to thrive and branch out in new directions. Everyone has his or her own favorite location, resort, and criteria for choosing a place to vacation. In this chapter, I give you my personal (and highly unscientific) recommendations for the hottest timeshare locations, top up-and-coming destinations, good-value spots, best family-friendly destinations, and popular places for retirees to vacation. I advise you on the best resorts, based on the annual top selections made by three separate (and highly recommended) timeshare consumer sources. Plus, I also help you understand the best reasons to buy timeshare in the first place — and the best reasons *not* to buy timeshare.

## Exploring the Best Reasons to Buy Timeshare

Buying timeshare is an entirely personal choice. For many people, it makes good sense, both budget-wise and as a lifestyle choice. For others, it's simply the wrong option. To see where you stand on the issue, take out a pencil and note "yes" or "no" next to the following scenarios:

✔ You like to plan in the long term. You want more security and peace of mind about your vacations and vacation accommodations in specific.

✔ You love going back to the same place every year to vacation.

✔ You can't afford to buy a complete condo, home, or other property, but you can afford to own a week or so of vacation time in a particular property.

✔ You like the idea of owning as opposed to renting, and see the value in such — whether using it for potential rental income or simply not having to book hotel rooms or rental units for each vacation.

✔ You like the idea of owning property that you don't have to personally maintain.

✔ Where costs are concerned, you like having few surprises. You like the fact that you're helping offset future vacation inflation. You like knowing what your vacation will cost, unlike quotes for hotel rates that often don't include extra fees and taxes (as high as 19% in some locales).

✔ You like having room enough to share your vacation space with family and friends.

Timeshare comes in all shapes, sizes, and costs, but the typical timeshare is a two-bedroom, two-bath unit with a living/dining room, full kitchen facilities, and a washer/dryer.

✔ You like the amenities that many timeshare resorts offer: complete recreational facilities (including golf courses, pools, tennis courts, gyms, and spas), maid service, laundry facilities, activities centers, shops, and restaurants.

✔ You love the idea of being able to exchange vacation weeks to destinations around the world.

✔ You want to leave a vacation legacy. Because the majority of timeshares in the United States are deeded and, therefore, willable, timeshare offers you the unique benefit of leaving this important legacy behind.

## Examining the Best Reasons Not to Buy Timeshare

If you answer "yes" to more than a few of the following, timeshare may not be for you:

✔ You're pressured into buying or you don't understand what you're buying.

✔ Your salesperson insults you. Unfortunately, this still happens in some resorts. I once overheard a salesperson ask his client, "Don't you feel stupid for spending $37,000 in hotels over the past 20 years?" I've heard sales managers from the old school of "sales via intimidation" make snide comments about the client's ability to afford the timeshare or the client's lack of understanding. My advice: If a salesperson or the sales manager insults you, find the person in charge and report it, and then leave.

✔ You prefer more flexibility in timing your vacations and choosing locations.

✔ You spend less than $500 per person per year on your vacations. Realistically, if you're spending less than $500 a year per person on vacations, it makes little economic sense to buy timeshare.

✔ You're buying it solely as a real estate investment. Even deeded in perpetuity, timeshare should not be bought as a real estate investment or under any other kind of investment strategy. It's an investment in your future vacations — period. And don't kid yourself into thinking that in ten years you will be able to sell your timeshare for substantially more than what you paid for it. You *may* be able to do that, but keep in mind that timeshare is not what I call "Donald Trump–style" real estate.

✔ You prefer to have your vacation property available for your use year-round.

✔ You love staying in hotels and trying out different hotels.

✔ You don't think you'll use it enough to make it worth the money. No matter what the price, no matter how desirable the property is, and no matter what the salesperson says, if you don't have the time to use it, don't buy it.

✔ You don't think it provides value in comparison with other vacations.

✔ You're not aware that maintenance fees can go up annually, and the resort may impose "special assessment" fees on occasion.

✔ You prefer to rent rather than own.

✔ You don't really have the money to spare. Buying timeshare shouldn't take food off your table, force you into mortgage foreclosure, stop you from paying your kid's college education, or in any way, shape, or form take away from the quality of your life.

## Homing in on the Top Timeshare Resorts

With more than 5,700 resorts worldwide, it can be difficult to say which timeshare resorts are the "best." But you can get a good indication of the gold standards of timeshare resorts from the lists made by the following three independent timeshare groups, who annually select what they consider to be the world's best timeshare resorts.

## Timeshare Users Group (TUG)

Timeshare Users Group, or TUG, as it is known (www.tug2.net), was founded in 1981 and is an online community of timeshare owners from around the world, with a heavy concentration of American owners. This independent consumer group collects reviews and ratings on timeshare resorts from members who've been there.

For 2004, TUG gave its best ratings to the resorts in Table 1-1.

### Table 1-1    Timeshare Users Group's Top Choices

| Rating | Resort | Location |
|--------|--------|----------|
| 10 | The Four Seasons | Scottsdale, Arizona |
| 10 | Residence Clubs at Troon North | Scottsdale, Arizona |
| 9.91 | The Four Seasons Resort Aviara | Carlsbad, California |
| 9.68 | Disney's Villas at the Wilderness Lodge | Orlando (Disney World), Florida |
| 9.68 | Royal Caribbean | Cancun, Mexico |
| 9.64 | Disney's Boardwalk Villas | Orlando (Disney World), Florida |
| 9.64 | Royal Islander | Cancun, Mexico |
| 9.60 | Royal Sands | Cancun, Mexico |
| 9.58 | Royal Mayan | Cancun, Mexico |
| 9.56 | Disney's Villas at Old Key West | Orlando (Disney World), Florida |
| 9.56 | St. James Place | Beaver Creek, Colorado |

## TimeSharing Today

*TimeSharing Today* (http://tstoday.com) is full of useful information on virtually all aspects of timesharing. Published every two months since 1991, *TimeSharing Today* isn't meant for the timeshare novice. Its readership and editorial staff are timeshare savvy, and the articles are well written and usually come directly from owners with solid, no-nonsense experience.

*TimeSharing Today* has been rating resorts since 1991, and all of its reviews are available online to subscribers of the magazine. The criteria for ratings include amenities and activities at the resort; amenities and activities nearby; the quality of the timeshare unit; its suitability for adults, kids, seniors, and physically disabled; and the quality of the resort facilities, security, and staff.

The resorts in Table 1-2 are the timeshare resorts receiving the highest scores from *TimeSharing Today:*

| Table 1-2 | *Timesharing Today's* Top Choices | |
|---|---|---|
| *Rating* | *Resort* | *Location* |
| 9.9 | The Four Seasons Residence Club Aviara | Carlsbad, California |
| 9.6 | Royal Islander | Cancun, Mexico |
| 9.6 | Chetola Resort | Blowing Rock, North Carolina |
| 9.6 | Fairfield Resort | Branson, Missouri |
| 9.5 | Marriott's Marbella Beach Resort | Marbella, Spain |
| 9.5 | Kona Coast Resort II | Kailua-Kona, Hawaii |
| 9.5 | Fairfield Resort | Nashville, Tennessee |
| 9.5 | Fairfield Resort | Old Town Alexandria, Virginia |
| 9.4 | Bay Club at Waikoloa Beach | Kamuela, Hawaii |
| 9.4 | Marriott's Custom House | Boston, Massachusetts |
| 9.4 | Marriott's Manor Club | Williamsburg, Virginia |
| 9.4 | Embassy Vacation Club | Poipu, Hawaii |

## *Hiatus Magazine*

This relatively new publication bills itself as a "Travel Magazine for Vacation & Timeshare Enthusiasts." *Hiatus* awards an "Editor's Choice Award" based on research and on-site reviews. *Hiatus* believes in maintaining a high degree of integrity by not mixing editorial (including reviews) with advertising. Basically that means that a resort doesn't have to spend any advertising dollars with the magazine in order to be reviewed and/or receive an "Editor's Choice Award."

Currently, *Hiatus* has evaluated timeshare resorts located only in Las Vegas, Orlando, Hawaii, Missouri, Arizona, and Spain. Those in Table 1-3 won its Editor's Choice Awards in 2004.

| Table 1-3 | *Hiatus* Magazine's Top Choices |
|---|---|
| *Resort* | *Location* |
| Cancun Resort–Monarch Grand Vacations | Las Vegas |
| Fairfield Grand Desert | Las Vegas |
| Disney's Beach Club Villas | Orlando, Florida |
| Disney's Boardwalk Villas | Orlando, Florida |
| Disney's Saratoga Springs Resort and Spa | Orlando, Florida |
| Fairfield Bonnet Creed | Orlando, Florida |
| Hilton Grand Vacations Club on International Drive | Orlando, Florida |
| Orange Lake Country Club | Orlando, Florida |
| Embassy Suites at Poipu Point | Kauai, Hawaii |
| Fairfield Kona Hawaiian Resort | Big Island, Hawaii |
| Hilton Grand Vacations Club at Hilton Hawaiian Village | Oahu, Hawaii |
| Marriott's Ko Olina Beach Club | Oahu, Hawaii |
| Marriott's Ocean Club | Maui, Hawaii |
| Marriott's Waiohai Beach Club | Kauai, Hawaii |
| Westin Ocean Villas | Maui, Hawaii |
| Worldmark by Trendwest | Maui, Hawaii |
| Big Cedar Wilderness Club | Branson, Missouri |
| Hyatt Pinon Pointe | Sedona, Arizona |
| California Beach Resort at Club La Costa | Malaga, Spain |

# Feeling the Heat of the Hottest Timeshare Destinations

Popular timeshare destinations tend to mirror popular hotel destinations. In the United States, Florida, California, and South Carolina have the most timeshare resorts — warm weather, beaches, and plenty of attractions make them obvious choices.

In Florida, Orlando has about 50% of the state's timeshare resorts, a constellation of rooms that revolve around that sun called Disney World. Las Vegas is getting bigger all the time, as evidenced by the number and size of the timeshare projects already there, as well as those in the works — including a massive project by Vegas entrepreneur Steve Wynn. Europeans, who take more (and longer) vacations than Americans, favor warm, sunny places that are easy to get to, like the Canary Islands. All in all, here are the hottest timeshare destinations at the moment:

- ✔ **Orlando, Florida**
- ✔ **Hilton Head Island, South Carolina**
- ✔ **Myrtle Beach, South Carolina**
- ✔ **Las Vegas**
- ✔ **Florida coasts** (both East and West)
- ✔ **California** (especially Southern California)
- ✔ **Hawaii**
- ✔ **Mexico** (Cancun and Puerto Vallarta, in particular)
- ✔ **Southern coast of Spain and the Canary Islands**
- ✔ **Southern Africa**
- ✔ **Rocky Mountain states (Colorado and Utah, in particular)**

# Paying Attention to Up-and-Coming Timeshare Destinations

In growing destinations, where demand for hotel rooms goes up, so does demand for timeshare. Here are some of the places where the market for timeshare is heating up:

- ✔ **U.S. Virgin Islands:** Unlike in some other Caribbean destinations, demand for timeshare in the Virgin Islands has been low until now, with timeshares popping up on the islands of St. Thomas and St. John.

- ✔ **The less popular Hawaiian Islands:** Timeshare is firmly entrenched in Maui and the Big Island, but now the smaller islands of Oahu and Molokai are getting in on the act.

- ✔ **Urban areas (United States and Europe):** Cities have one big obstacle when it comes to timeshare — limited space — but *urban interval ownership* is becoming increasingly popular in places like San Francisco, Boston, and New York (see Chapter 16).

- ✔ **India and China:** As these countries have become hot-ticket destinations, timeshare has followed, with units opening up in places like Bangalore and Goa (in India) and Shanghai and Hong Kong (in China).

- ✔ **Napa Valley:** Timeshare is growing in this haven of spa resorts and boutique inns.

- ✔ **British Columbia/Vancouver:** This photogenic region is increasingly a destination for timeshare buyers.

# Budgeting for Good-Value Timeshare Destinations

It's almost sacrilege for a timeshare salesperson like me to say, but if you're looking for bargain timeshare, buying resale is often your best bet. Still, you can often find good value in new timeshares that are located in destinations that have the following characteristics:

- ✔ The industry is just getting off the ground in a particular location.

- ✔ The timeshare is located in an off-the-beaten-path spot where demand is relatively low.

- ✔ The timeshare is in a place with a glut of timeshare offerings (such as Cancun).

- ✔ The location has favorable exchange rates, inexpensive land costs, and/or low property taxes.

Getting "good value" is also about what matters to you. For some consumers, it may mean a $60,000 three-bedroom condo used during Christmas week (high season) in Vail, Colorado. For others, it may mean a week in a $10,000 two-bedroom condo in the middle of Minnesota in October (low season). Good value has more to do with what you intend to do with your timeshare than with the price you pay. For more on determining good value when buying timeshare, go to Chapter 4.

If you're looking for destinations where deals are still to be had, check out the following:

- ✔ **South Africa**
- ✔ **Beaches on the Florida Panhandle**
- ✔ **South Carolina inland**
- ✔ **Minnesota** (during nonski season)
- ✔ **Cancun**

# Taking the Kids to Family-Friendly Timeshare Destinations

Orlando, Florida, leads the list of family-friendly vacation destinations for the sheer number of things to do with the family while on vacation. There are approximately 90 timeshare resorts within the Orlando area. Beach areas are extremely popular with families as well, although areas such as Hilton Head Island are less popular with families and more popular among adults, particularly adults who golf.

- ✔ **Orlando, Florida**
- ✔ **Florida coasts** (both East and West)
- ✔ **Colorado** and other Rockies ski destinations
- ✔ **Missouri**
- ✔ **Urban areas,** such as New York City and San Francisco (although urban areas have a smaller number of timeshare resorts — see Chapter 16)
- ✔ **Texas** (especially beach areas like Galveston)
- ✔ **Williamsburg, Virginia**
- ✔ **The Caribbean** (for families who can afford the airfare, or for those families adding a week of timeshare to a cruise vacation)

# Finding the Top Timeshare Destinations for Retirees

Although no one actually uses their timeshare(s) for strictly retirement living, an increasing number of consumers are able to vacation more in their retirement, particularly if they purchase their timeshare when they're still working, when they can more easily afford the payments.

Most retirees are looking for quiet, less crowded destinations, like the little out-of-the-way cabins found in the Wisconsin Dells, or a beachfront condo during the relatively low-key months of May or September.

Some of the most popular choices for retirees include

- ✔ **Arizona**
- ✔ **Marco Island, Florida**
- ✔ **Upper Midwest**
- ✔ **England and Italy** (both of which have a high number of timeshare destinations)
- ✔ **Colorado** (except during ski season)
- ✔ **Pacific Northwest and Canada** (except during ski season)

# Chapter 2

# Digging Deeper into Timeshare

*In This Chapter*

▶ Discovering the meaning of "timeshare"

▶ Discussing the types of timeshare ownerships and uses

▶ Exchanging your timeshare

*I*n writing *Timeshare For Dummies,* 1st Edition, it's my utmost goal to present both the pros and the cons of buying timeshare. In this chapter, I lay out the basic principles of timeshare: What is timeshare? What types of properties are out there? How you can use and exchange yours?

## *What Is Timeshare?*

*Timeshare,* in its simplest definition, is a joint ownership or lease of vacation property by several people who take turns occupying the premises for fixed periods. In other words, timeshare is nothing more than a group of people sharing the cost of a vacation place. Think of it as buying your future vacations at today's prices.

In the old days, timeshare product generally consisted of condominium units. These days, timeshare are that and more: a hotel room, a cabin, a house, a castle, a treehouse, a chalet, a boat, a yacht, and even a jet.

Timeshare is sold in many ways: by referral, by resale, over the Internet, even on eBay. But the main way timeshare is still sold and marketed is through on-site **sales presentations.**

 In the interest of full disclosure, let me say this: I am a timeshare salesperson. I know what you'll hear from the staff at a timeshare sales presentation. In introducing the concept of timeshare to clients, timeshare salespeople typically present the following chart, asking, "Which makes more sense for you?"

## You say it's vacation ownership, I say it's timeshare

Many timeshare resorts and operators feel that the word "timeshare" still conjures up a sleazy image to many consumers. I can't tell you how many timeshare operations don't even mention the word "timeshare" anymore — and I'm talking even the giant companies. The major brands try their mightiest to distance themselves from the term. Disney Vacation Club never uses the word timeshare in its printed materials or during its sales presentations. A spokesperson for Hyatt said, "When you're spending $130,000 [for one of its luxury fractional timeshare products], you don't want to call it timeshare." A salesperson at a Sheraton timeshare property even told me, "I own timeshare, and our product is *not* timeshare."

What you hear instead are so-called softer terms, such as "vacation ownership" and "vacation clubs."

| *Renting* | *Owning* |
|---|---|
| Rent receipts | Deed and title |
| No equity | Equity |
| No tax advantages | Possible tax advantages |
| Basic 350-square-foot hotel room | Large space with kitchen facilities |
| Nothing to pass on in your will | Vacation legacy to pass on |
| Less control of vacation costs | More control of vacation costs |

Looks like a no-brainer, right? Before you jump into buying on the spot, however, read on as I break down the many variables that may arise from that simple comparison chart. Obviously, not all hotel rooms are only 350 square feet, and not all timeshares are more spacious than all hotel rooms. Not all timeshares come with a deed. And yes, although your costs are largely fixed when you buy timeshare, maintenance costs and taxes can go up annually, and you may be hit with special assessment fees from time to time.

Pitting timeshares against hotel rooms or full ownership property is not the issue. It's really all about how you prefer to vacation. If you don't think you're going to use timeshare, don't buy it, no matter what the price, no matter how desirable the property is, and no matter what the salesperson says.

## The art of the scam

Timeshare may have cleaned up its act considerably, but it is still a business, and in any business where big money is involved, creative crooks are on the scene with new twists on old scams. Fortunately, their mischief is usually short-lived, thanks to tighter regulations, watchdog groups, and increasingly savvier consumers. Check out Chapter 17 for examples of timeshare hustles and hucksterisms.

Suppose you want to vacation in the south of France next year for one week. What are your choices? Here are several vacation options:

- ✔ **Rent a hotel room for a week.** Simple. You've rented hotel rooms your whole life, and so have your parents. You pay money and room tax to rent the hotel room. Out of this money, the hotel pays for the room, the labor, and the maintenance and derives a profit.

- ✔ **Rent a condo or house for a week.** Pretty much the same premise as renting a hotel room: You pay to rent, and the owner of the condo or house recoups his cost, pays for the labor and the maintenance, and derives a profit.

- ✔ **Buy a house outright.** You pay the cost of the complete house and any taxes, as well as all the maintenance and labor on the house. Plus, if you intend to use it only sporadically, you have the added responsibility of finding someone to rent it the remaining weeks of the year. This may turn out to be a smart investment, but it requires a lot of money upfront — an option many vacationers simply can't afford.

Or . . .

- ✔ **Buy a week of timeshare at a vacation spot that allows you to go to the south of France this year, Gatlinburg, Tennessee, the next year, and somewhere else the year after that.** Yes, you're paying the cost of the room, as well as the labor to maintain it, and the owner of the resort is making a profit. But you don't have to pay exorbitant upfront costs, you have a deed rather than a rental receipt, and you're guaranteed a week of vacation at your home resort or exchange resort every year. And if you have a large family, buying timeshare with more than one bedroom is a smart way to offset the costs of shelling out for multiple hotel rooms.

## Discovering the Types of Timeshare Ownerships

Timeshare is not *whole ownership,* like a vacation or second home. There are three basic types of timeshare ownership scenarios:

✓ **Fee-simple:** In *fee-simple,* or *deeded timeshare,* you purchase an actual deeded interest in real estate that is then recorded with the court or other authorities in the place where you purchased. You receive a title in perpetuity, which means you should have the rights to use, rent, lend, will, and sell your share of the property as you see fit. It's always a good idea to ask before signing whether you're getting the full bundle of rights.

✓ **Leasehold:** A *leasehold timeshare* (a type of *nondeeded* timeshare property) is very similar to a fee-simple timeshare; the major difference is that a leasehold is *not* in perpetuity. Rather, a leasehold has a specified expiration date that may be at the end of a given year or a given number of usages.

✓ **Right-to-use:** A *right-to-use timeshare* (another type of nondeeded timeshare property) gives you the right to use a particular unit or unit size each year, but you have no actual real estate interest. Most right-to-use timeshares are similar to leasehold timeshares in that the majority have a stated expiration date. Generally, these types of timeshares are held by a trust company; many timeshares outside the United States are typically right-to-use.

Confused? Fee-simple, or deeded timeshare property, is similar in many ways to deeded property in anything else. You own it; it's yours. The vast majority of deeded property is deeded in perpetuity — that is, forever. However, because of legal restrictions in some areas, some deeded timeshare is deeded for only 99 years.

Leasehold and right-to-use timeshare are examples of nondeeded timeshare property. This type of timeshare is owned not in perpetuity but for a specific number or years or a specific number of uses.

One is not necessarily better than the other. For example, the Disney Vacation Club (DVC) is nondeeded. This is a specific-number-of-years, right-to-use product. You may, however, sell, rent, or will your DVC usage just as you would your deeded timeshare, but keep in mind that any usages expire at the designated time. On the other hand, the Manhattan Club in New York City is fully deeded. You own your share of the property (your unit) forever. Of course, timeshare is still relatively new. What will happen to that one-bedroom suite at the Manhattan Club in the year 2042 remains to be seen.

## Using Your Timeshare

Within the three basic types of timeshare ownership, there are four ways to use your timeshare. For more using your timeshare, go to Chapter 16.

✓ **Fixed week:** This is the simplest type of timeshare. It gives you rights to a specific week of the year, for a specific room size, more likely than not at a specific resort that you return to year after year (defined as your *home resort*), or trade or exchange using whichever trading company your home resort is affiliated with, for a similar room in a similarly rated resort (generally for a fee). Sometimes you may be able to exchange for a different week of the year, for yet another fee.

The greatest advantage to the fixed week system is that if you know you will be going to use your home resort during a specific week of the year, your condo will be there for you at your home resort, no reservations necessary.

✔ **Floating week:** Also referred to as *flex week*. Buying a floating week gives you rights to one week during the year to be used at your home resort or an affiliated resort (generally for a fee). Note that floating or flex weeks are usually allocated by season at your home resort.

Having floating week timeshare gives you more flexibility in terms of using it but places greater responsibilities on you, because you must always reserve your week ahead of time, sometimes months in advance.

✔ **Points:** In a points-based system, each week of timeshare owned is allocated a specific number of points, based on such criteria as size of condo, rating of resort, and the like. Although there are exceptions, the majority of points-based timeshares have their deeds held in trust by the developer, *not* the owner.

The greatest advantage to points is that the owner is not locked into a full week; more often than not, two- and three-day stays are permissible. For example, if it requires 1,000 points to stay the full week, it may require only 350 points to stay on a Monday and Tuesday, leaving 650 points to be used at a later date. Some, but not all, points-based systems can be used to round out your vacation, meaning they can be used for airline tickets, car rentals, hotels, cruises, and even some theme-park tickets.

The greatest disadvantage (and it's a big one) to a points-based system is that more often than not, the points are not inflation proof. What does that mean? Say your two-bedroom timeshare is worth 100,000 points. This year, it may take 100,000 points to trade or exchange for a two-bedroom condo in the south of France. Then next year comes around, and the trading company requires 150,000 points for the same condo. It's no wonder that some skeptics have posited that the points-based system was designed solely to consistently require consumers to spend more money to purchase more points.

Always ask whether points are inflation-proof points before signing paperwork. For more on points, see Chapter 12.

✔ **Fractionals/private residence clubs (PRC):** Fractionals are the fastest-growing segment of the timeshare industry, and the most costly. In *fractionals,* the purchaser owns a large number of weeks (typically ¼, ⅙, or ⅓ of the year, which is how "fractionals" got their name). Timeshares that operate as fractionals are typically run by management companies and have sizeable annual maintenance fees as well as membership fees.

Private residence clubs (PRC) are usually ultraluxurious properties found in the most desired locations around the world. They may come complete with automobiles, private chefs, and full-time personal assistants and offer many of the same amenities as country clubs. People with cash to burn are gobbling up fractionals and PRCs rapidly. For more on fractionals, go to Chapter 16.

## Exchanging Your Timeshare

Your home resort is the destination you return to year after year. Some people prefer to vacation only in their home resort with no variation. But for many other people, timeshare is especially attractive because of the exchange factor: You have the chance to stay in a different place in the world every year. Timeshare exchange companies allow timeshare owners to trade their week with a timeshare week in a different location.

Keep in mind that exchange companies prefer that trades are generally "like for like," and rank high demand/low demand destinations with devices like color codes and industry ratings. It may be hard to trade your week in a low-demand resort during the low season for a high-demand resort in high season, although it can happen — and it's all a matter of personal preference and flexibility anyway. Orlando, Florida, may be as high demand as a destination can be (and it doesn't get any hotter), but that doesn't necessarily mean you want to vacation there.

Even though you may be purchasing your timeshare with the express purpose of trading or exchanging, the mantra in timeshare is this:

> *The power of your exchange is dependent solely on what you put into the system, not what you take out.*

In other words, the power of your exchange is dependent on how desirable your timeshare week is to other traders. For more on exchanging and the two major exchange companies, Resort Condominiums International (RCI) and Interval International (II), turn to Chapter 12.

## Sizing Up Your Options

One big determination for potential timeshare buyers is making sure the timeshare unit is large enough to accommodate your needs — or, paradoxically, making sure you don't buy more space than you actually plan to use. Timeshare units range from efficiencies or studios that sleep two people to houses with four or more bedrooms that can comfortably sleep 12 or more people. The resort directories for both II and RCI exchange companies differentiate between *private sleeping capacity* and *total sleeping capacity*.

- ✔ **Total sleeping capacity** is the number of people than the timeshare unit can sleep in total, meaning that someone may be sleeping on a sleeper sofa in the living room, which is not private.

- ✔ **Private sleeping capacity** is just that: separate sleeping rooms. II uses icons to show that the unit in question is, for example, a two-bedroom that sleeps four privately and six in total. RCI simply uses a slash: 6/4.

Another feature about timeshare unit size is whether the unit can be split up. The common term for a timeshare unit that can be split into separate usages is a *lockout* or a *lock-off* unit. Lock-off units are units that can be split into two or more separate units or combined into one large unit. For example, a two-bedroom unit can be used for either one week every year in a two-bedroom unit or two weeks every year each in a one-bedroom unit.

Some units are actual physical lockouts. For example, a two-bedroom unit may consist of two separate one-bedrooms, connected by a door that can be locked out (hence the terms lock-off or lockout). Other units are one unit consisting of two bedrooms (and generally two baths) and one living/eating area. Those units may not be physical lock-offs, but the resort may still allow you to convert a two-bedroom into two separate one-bedroom units.

Always ask whether you'll need to pay a fee to split up your weeks, no matter what the physical unit looks like. Make sure to also ask whether a two-bedroom unit will split or convert into two full one-bedrooms. Often, resorts will allow a split, but what the owner ends up with is a one-bedroom one week and a studio the next, not two weeks of full one-bedroom units.

Most resorts offer timeshare purchases on an annual or biannual (every other year) basis. Some resorts even offer triannual ownership.

In most cases, the cost of a three-bedroom timeshare will be lower than the cost of buying three separate one-bedroom timeshare units, and the cost per week will be even lower if you have full lockout capabilities. For example, Sue and Doug vacation three weeks each year by themselves. If they purchase three separate one-bedroom timeshare units, their expenses might look like this:

Timeshare #1: $9,000 + Annual maintenance and taxes ($350)

Timeshare #2: $9,000 + Annual maintenance and taxes ($350)

Timeshare #3: $9,000 + Annual maintenance and taxes ($350)

Effective cost per week: $9,350

But if Sue and Doug purchase one three-bedroom timeshare unit with full lockout capability (meaning it could be used for three separate one-bedroom stays each year), their expenses might look like this:

Timeshare #1  $20,000 + Annual Maintenance and Taxes ($700)

Effective cost per week: $6,900

Never buy more than you think you're going to use, unless money is of no concern to you. The best value is often a three-bedroom lockout annual that can be used for three weeks each in a one-bedroom condo. But if you aren't going to need three weeks a year, don't buy it!

# History 101: The main events

Of the two once-upon-a-time versions of the story of timeshare, Version One goes something like this: In September 1963, in Baar, Switzerland, Alexander Nette and his colleague Guido M. Fenggli came up with a way to give vacationers access to rent-free holidays every year. They set up a company called Hapimag (Hotel und Appartementhaus Immobilient Aniage AG), the members of which could spend time in their own vacation property without being tied down to a single destination or having to invest a large sum of money. Soon after, Mr. Nette began to acquire properties in various resorts throughout Europe, in countries like Italy, Spain, and Switzerland. These properties were made available to the public on a *right-to-use basis* — that is, no deeds were made available and no one had full ownership.

Forty years later, Hapimag (www.hapimag.com/wps/portal) continues to thrive as an independent company, with more than 60 holiday resorts in 18 European countries, the United States, and Egypt.

Version Two of the story is that sometime between 1964 and 1968, Paul Doumier of the Societe des Grandes Travaux de Marseille, a development company in France, created the concept for a ski resort located in the French Alps. Mr. Doumier was the person who came up with the timeshare selling pitch, still in widespread use today, that says that it is cheaper "to buy the hotel than rent the room."

Skip ahead to 1969 when the first timeshare was sold in the United States. It was sold as a *leasehold* (again, no full ownership) on Kauai in Hawaii. These units were sold as a 40-year lease, in one-week increments, a practice that has not varied considerably in more than 30 years.

In 1973, timeshare came of age and entered the *deeded* era — wherein buyers have legal ownership of the timeshare property, giving them the same rights of ownership as other deeded real estate (they are entitled to sell, rent, will, or give away the property). Brockway Springs in Lake Tahoe, California, claims that it sold the first fully deeded timeshare. More important, the gentlemen behind this deal — Carl Berry, Paul Gray, Greg Bright, Doug Murdock, and Dave Irmer — brought the concept of time-sharing to the financial world and also labeled the product *timeshare*.

# Chapter 3

# Understanding the Basic Economics of Timeshare

● ● ● ● ● ● ● ● ● ● ● ● ● ● ● ● ● ● ● ● ● ● ● ● ● ● ● ● ● ● ● ● ● ● ● ● ● ● ● ● ●

## In This Chapter

▶ Breaking down the costs of timeshare

▶ Adding up the extra fees

▶ Finding ways to cut costs or actually snag a bargain

● ● ● ● ● ● ● ● ● ● ● ● ● ● ● ● ● ● ● ● ● ● ● ● ● ● ● ● ● ● ● ● ● ● ● ● ● ● ● ● ●

*T*his chapter looks at the basic economics of timeshare. Keep in mind that timesharing is nothing more than an alternative to spending money on renting a hotel, motel, condo, cabin, or house. Owning timeshare, however, gives you equity and the ability to purchase additional weeks of vacation (starting at around $149 a week) to exchange for like properties around the world, and to rent, sell, or have something to leave to your grandchildren.

Timeshare is never free; don't ever get into timeshare hoping you'll be able to vacation for free at some point.

## Buying Timeshare: Making an Informed Choice

At its best, timeshare is a reallocation of money that you would already be spending on vacation accommodations. The two following sections give you a couple of sample scenarios that show how buying timeshare measures up financially in the short and long runs.

### Example #1: One week of vacation per year

This is a scenario for people who use one week a year in a one-bedroom/one-bath timeshare.

# The booming business of timeshare

Timeshare continues to grow and thrive, even in rocky economic climates. *The Wall Street Journal* reported that net sales of timeshares hit a record $5.5 billion in the United States in 2003, up 34% from that sold in 2002. A timeshare week sold for an average $14,500 in the U.S., with the average maintenance fee at around $385 for each week of use.

Timeshare is a booming business, but the good news for consumers is that it's also a *cleaner* business. These days, consumers are much more aware of what they're getting when they sign on the dotted line. The buzzword in timeshare contracting these days is *transparency*, which means getting full disclosure of what you're purchasing — a big positive for an industry that once operated in the murky world of smoke-and-mirrors selling.

| | |
|---|---|
| Purchase price | $10,000 |
| Down payment | $1,000 |
| Amount financed | $9,000 |
| Interest rate | 15.9% |
| Term | 7 Years |
| Monthly payment | $178.24 × 84 monthly payments |
| Amount paid | $14,972.16 |

Remember that timeshare means you're paying now (or for the term of your loan) for your future vacations. So, that leaves you with the following:

✔ If you use your timeshare for the one week per year for only the seven years of the term, you pay $2,138.88 per week of vacation accommodations, or $305.55 per night. Quite a bit more than if you're paying $59.99 for your vacation accommodations now.

✔ If you use your timeshare for the one-week per year for ten years, you pay $1,497.21 per week of vacation accommodations, or $213.88 per night. Again, much higher than the $59.99 you're paying today, but better than the first example.

✔ If, like most people who eventually become owners, you use your timeshare for the one-week per year for 20 years, you end up paying $748.60 per week of vacation accommodations, or $106.94 per night.

## *Example #2: Two weeks of vacation per year*

This is a scenario for people who vacation for two weeks a year, so I use a two-bedroom/two-bath timeshare, which can be split into two weeks each in a one-bedroom timeshare.

| | |
|---|---|
| Purchase price | $17,000 |
| Down payment | $1,700 |
| Amount financed | $15,300 |
| Interest rate | 15.9% |
| Term | 7 Years |
| Monthly payment | $301.01 × 84 monthly payments |
| Amount paid | $25,284.84 |

✔ Seven years of vacation yields $3,612.12 for two weeks of vacation, or $258.00 per night.

✔ Ten years of vacation yields $2,528.48 for two weeks of vacation, or $180.60 per night.

✔ Twenty years of vacation yields $1,264.24 for two weeks of vacation, or $90.30 per night — a very good deal in 20 years!

## A family affair

For many families, timeshare is an attractive vacation option, and often makes good economic sense. According to AAA, the average family of four spends $244 per day for lodging, meals, taxes, and gratuities on vacation. For a one-week vacation, that can really add up. Here are some examples of the average vacation costs for a family of four:

Hawaii: $532.66 per day

Washington, D.C.: $380.33

Rhode Island: $314.20

New York: $304.09

Massachusetts: $301.94

Florida: $283.75

Kansas: $182.55

South Dakota: $180.90

Oklahoma: $180.85

For just about the same amount of money, a family can vacation in Hawaii, California, Florida, or even Australia and stay in a Five-Star timeshare resort with two or three bedrooms, a full kitchen (saving money on eating out), and recreational amenities at no extra cost. And they could do so year after year and own a deed and title as well.

The salesperson has been trained, as have all salespeople, to involve you emotionally, often talking about the beauty of the resort, the many amenities, and how buying timeshare has changed some people's lives. You, as the consumer, are in the driver's seat, so don't let emotion get in the way of logic.

Sometimes, however, emotion trumps logic. I once sold a timeshare to an 87-year-old man and his 85-year-old wife. Obviously, everyone knew that they weren't going to be able to get 20 years' use out of their timeshare. Before the gentleman began to fill out the paperwork, I gently asked him why he decided to purchase. He looked up at me and said, "Lisa, I am 87 years old and my wife is 85. We both worked for more than 50 years and we've never gone on a first-class vacation. Even if we only use this timeshare once, we deserve to go first class." It was a romantic notion and a bold move, and he wouldn't be talked out of it.

## Breaking Down the Costs

Costs for timeshare units run the gamut these days: Upscale "fractionals" have hit the high six figures, while the average cost for a timeshare condo in 2004 is settling around $13,500. The following is a sample chart showing the breakdown of costs for a typical timeshare transaction.

### Sample Pricing for a Three-Bedroom Unit

| | |
|---|---|
| Purchase price | $21,900 |
| First-day incentive | $2,000 |
| Closing costs | $600 |
| 20% down payment | $4,590 |
| Monthly payment | $386.29 |

*(Calculated at 15.9% interest for five years)*

Now I break down the elements of the preceding table.

### Purchase price

Some developers and salespeople use inflated figures to start, in order to test your temperature and your willingness to purchase. It's unfortunate, but it does happen. Then, if you're hesitant or express concern about the price, the salesperson leans in and says something like, "You know, we can do better here" and a couple of thousand is lopped off the price — a little trick known in timeshare industry as *the drop*. My motto is, "the price is the price is the price"; playing price games with potential buyers seemed like a waste of both our time. However, it never hurts to ask whether a lower price is available.

## Down payment

Many timeshares show (as does the preceding example) a down payment of 20%. In most cases, however, the *standard industry down payments* are 10% — and in some cases, even lower. Financing rates are typically very high; for example, as of the writing of this book, typical resort financing rates are about 15.9%, when the average mortgage rates are about 6%.

## Interest

What? 15.9% interest? Unfortunately, yes. The interest rate is so high because anyone who walks into a timeshare immediately "qualifies" for the company's financing. So you, the consumer, pay the price for this everyone-qualifies deal.

## First-day incentives

Most timeshares offer you a *first-day incentive* as a bonus for making the purchase right there on the spot. These incentives can be as varied as a price discount, membership fees waived for the first year (or longer), a lower financing rate, extra vacation time, additional attraction tickets, free or deeply discounted cruises, owners' parties, free meals while you're on vacation, and the like. Are these incentives legal? Yes, they are. There is nothing to prevent a timeshare resort from offering you deals to purchase today.

For more information, go to Chapter 8.

 Being a single person who enjoys vacationing, I find that timeshare saves me more money than it may a couple or family. Why? Simple: Most hotels, motels, condos, and the like mark up room rates sometimes by as much as 175% for a *single supplement* (the fee the lodging charges for a single person to use a room). So by owning timeshare, I avoid having to pay single-supplement fees.

# Uncovering Additional Fees

It's a myth to think that after the timeshare is paid off, you don't have to shell out any more money. This section discusses the extra fees that most timeshare owners can expect to pay annually.

## Maintenance fees

In most cases, timeshares access a monthly or yearly maintenance fee. Maintenance fees vary quite a bit by region, type of resort, type of ownership, and brand of timeshare, but this fee averages $500 per year for a two-bedroom timeshare in the United States.

Owners share both the use and the operating costs of the upkeep of their unit and the common grounds. These fees usually cover such expenses as resort management, upkeep and refurbishing of the individual rooms or condos, utilities, maintenance and upkeep of the common areas of the resort (swimming pools, tennis courts, and golf courses), and, in the case of deeded timeshare, real estate taxes.

Individual maintenance fees quoted may or may not include real estate taxes, so be sure to check with the resort policy. Also expect maintenance fees to go up periodically throughout the lifetime of the timeshare. Just as you pay more to maintain your house year after year, the older a resort gets, the more it costs to keep up the maintenance. Find out what the fees are this year, what they were the previous year, and what, if any, is the *cap*, or the legal limit, that they can be raised. What seems like a bargain at $350 a year may not be such a bargain in ten years if there is no cap and the fees go up 15% per year!

Keep in mind that a higher maintenance fee does not always translate into a better timeshare resort. If you aren't a golfer, for example, why buy at a resort that has a golf course, especially if you'll be staying in your home resort more than exchanging it?

Yes, maintenance fees can and do increase over the years. But they can also decrease at times, although this is rare and can sometimes signal problems with the resort.

Generally, maintenance fees at timeshare resorts cover:

- ✔ Normal wear and tear
- ✔ Upkeep of units and grounds
- ✔ Periodic painting
- ✔ Furniture and fixture repair and/or replacement
- ✔ Property insurance
- ✔ Liability insurance
- ✔ Minimum housekeeping of each occupied unit

Generally, maintenance fees at timeshare resorts do *not* cover:

- ✔ Abuse of property and/or fixtures
- ✔ Additions to units and/or grounds
- ✔ Extraordinary repairs due to weather

Although some timeshares allow you to roll maintenance fees into your monthly payment, rather than present you with a bill once a year, I strongly advise you to ask to see these fees separately from your monthly payment, so you know exactly how they break down.

Before you consider buying at a timeshare resort, ask the following questions about the types of fees you will be accessed:

> ✔ What is covered and what is not covered?
>
> ✔ What is the total amount?
>
> ✔ What were the fees last year and the year before that?
>
> ✔ Is there a limit, or cap, on these fees?
>
> ✔ Who, if anyone, votes on these fees? Are timeshare owners included on the voting board?
>
> ✔ Are these fees charged every year even though you, for example, own the timeshare only every other year?

I've read articles that advise potential owners to ask for and read the entire operating-expenses report for the resort before purchasing anything. This is not necessary. While you should always get straightforward answers to the questions listed, it's simply not necessary to go over the books with a fine-tooth comb.

### Property taxes

In cases where you actually own deeded property, you may also have to pay property taxes. Sometimes, these fees are called *annual dues* or *yearly upkeep*. Whatever they're called, ask questions about these fees and consider the long-term implications of paying them.

Laws governing these taxes vary from state to state and jurisdiction to jurisdiction. However, the issue most consumers are most interested in is the potential deductibility of the property taxes. Unfortunately, there is no easy or one-size-fits-all answer to this question.

The answer depends on such variables as:

> ✔ Whether you own a home
>
> ✔ What state you live in
>
> ✔ How many weeks of timeshare you currently own
>
> ✔ How much you currently earn
>
> ✔ Whether you're putting the deed in your name or in a company's name

Property taxes on a deeded timeshare are tax deductible provided you already own a home and you're not already taking a similar deduction on more than three weeks of timeshare.

### Miscellaneous fees

In addition to maintenance fees and property taxes, timeshare owners may face the possibility of having to pay one or more of the following fees at some point.

✔ **Special assessments:** Resort operators sometimes require owners to pay special assessment fees to offset the costs of major maintenance overhauls. Also note that in most seaside, beachside, or lakeside resorts, as well as in golf resorts, an annual or periodic special assessment is assessed to cover natural beach erosion, higher-than-average upkeep, damage from storms, and the like. Always ask — and if you're concerned about special assessments, a waterfront or golf resort may not be the best buy for you.

✔ **Activity or service fees:** These are fees associated with various activities at or services offered by the resort. For example: You may get free tennis court time, but you may have to rent equipment, like rackets. Always find out exactly what amenities are available to you at no cost and what extra costs may be involved.

✔ **Utility surcharges:** This is a potential charge for electricity, water, gas, and phone, and it's pretty rare. Most resorts include all but phone charges in the annual maintenance fees. Utility surcharges are applied when a particular utility (for example, electricity in California several years ago) experiences a sharp hike in price.

✔ **Bed tax:** This is another rarely applied fee. The fee that RCI and Interval International (known as II) charge to exchange is inclusive of taxes, unlike a hotel, which will charge not only the room fee but a hotel/bed tax (19% in Manhattan) to boot. The resort may even try to impose a bed tax for extras like rollaway beds and cribs. I don't like these fees. Owners and exchangers should *not* be charged any tax on the exchange fee.

# Looking for Ways to Cut Costs or Find Bargains

If you're a creative type, you can probably find ways to chip away at the cost of timeshare. The following savvy cost-cutting tips come from *TimeSharing Today* (www.timesharingtoday.com), a solid, independent online timeshare magazine with more than two million subscribers (see Chapter 1).

## Cutting costs

During your time at development sales centers or after sales presentations, ask your salesperson about discounts for:

✔ A special first-day incentive if you buy immediately following the initial presentation.

✔ An all-cash payment.

✔ A down payment larger than the standard 10%.

✔ A quantity discount if you buy more than one unit-week, or more than a certain number of points in a vacation club.

✔ Electronic funds transfer of monthly payments from your checking account or credit card.

✔ Resale of a previously owned product.

As a courtesy to owners who want or need to sell, some developers operate a resale program. At a resort being built in phases over a period of years, you may pay less for a resale unit-week in an older section of the resort, where your accommodations won't be brand-new and may lack certain amenities and refinements present in the newer units.

✔ Resorts with unsold units in less-than-prime locations.

Instead of a golf course or ocean view, you may be looking out at an interior courtyard — or the garbage dumpster. Your salesperson should be especially flexible in negotiating prices for such accommodations.

✔ Purchase of a new unit-week in a phase or at a resort approaching sellout. With just a scattering of unsold unit-weeks remaining in units of varying sizes, sales become more difficult, so many developers offer discounts to move the remaining inventory quickly.

## Finding resale bargains

In addition to developers' sales centers, you may also be able to find bargains by looking into resale. Check out the following and flip to Chapter 9 for more information on buying resale.

✔ **Classified advertising:** Look in newspapers and timeshare-related consumer publications, such as *TimeSharing Today* (www.time sharingtoday.com), and on Web sites, including **Timeshare Resale Alliance** (www.resaletimeshare.com) and **Timeshare Tips** (www.tstips.com).

✔ **Mature resorts with resales:** The owners' association may be assisting owners who want to resell and/or trying to sell timeshares it acquired through foreclosure from owners who failed to pay maintenance fees and property taxes.

✔ **Independent real-estate brokers:** In some resort areas, certain brokers specialize in timeshare resales.

✔ **Timeshare auctions:** TRI West Timeshare in Los Angeles (www.triwest-timeshare.com) sells close to a hundred resale time-shares a year at an annual auction. Online, timeshares also may be available at auction sites such as eBay (see Chapter 9) and Yahoo!.

# Do the split

*Lock-off units* are units that can be split into two or more separate units or combined into one large unit. Owning a lock-off unit is like getting two weeks for one. Generally speaking, if you own a lock-off unit, you can use that unit for two weeks of vacationing. You can, for example, use a week at the resort and exchange a week someplace else. If you own a two-bedroom lock-off, it may also be divided into a one bedroom and a studio, or some other configuration. A lock-off unit can increase the trading power of the unit. For more on lock-offs, see Chapter 2.

# Chapter 4

# Is Timeshare Right for You?

*In This Chapter*
▶ Discussing the most frequently asked questions about timeshare
▶ Pinpointing foolish assumptions
▶ Zeroing in on the issues every consumer should understand

*U*se this chapter as a sort of timeshare cheat sheet, where I lay out the basic concept of timeshare, the pros and cons of buying timeshare, the foolish assumptions you never want to make about timeshare, and the top consumer concerns.

## Answering the Most Frequently Asked Questions about Timeshare

As a timeshare salesperson, I have always strongly encouraged people to ask questions during the presentation. I end the *discovery* (questioning) period of my presentations by asking attendees whether they have any questions or concerns about the product, the company, or myself that need to be answered in order to make an intelligent, educated choice. Here, then, are the basic questions I encounter most frequently from clients.

You have every right to have your salesperson answer any questions you have about timeshare.

### What is timeshare?

In the simplest terms, *timeshare* allows you to purchase, either under deeded or nondeeded ownership (see Chapter 2), a certain amount of time you can use to take a vacation. Generally, timeshares are purchased and used in resort-type accommodations. Depending on the type of timeshare, owners may exchange or trade their accommodations, split larger accommodations into smaller accommodations for longer periods of time, or take advantage of myriad other benefits offered by either the resort or the exchange company with which the resort is affiliated.

## What's the difference between timeshare and vacation ownership?

In truth, nothing. Many timeshare resorts and operators feel that for many consumers "timeshare" still holds images of slick salesmen in lime-green leisure suits selling swampland to innocent victims. Some timeshare operations don't even mention the word "timeshare" anymore — and that includes the big names. Instead, you'll hear softer terms such as *vacation club* or *vacation ownership*. But a rose by any other name. . . .

## Can I sell my timeshare if I don't want it anymore?

Yes, in most cases you will be able to sell it. A word of caution here, however: Don't expect to make money selling your timeshare. Although many timeshares are, in fact, real estate, it should not be thought of as Donald Trump–type real estate. If you purchase a timeshare today for $13,000 (the average price in the United States), you probably can't turn around and sell it in five years for $20,000. In fact, 99 times out of 100, you can't and won't. So although you probably won't earn a profit from selling your timeshare, compare your possible ROI (return on investment) with any money you could make by selling your hotel and motel receipts after ten years — which is $0.

## How much should I pay for timeshare?

This is a difficult question to answer. Costs for timeshare vary widely based on the following criteria:

- Where the timeshare is located
- Whether the timeshare is deeded in perpetuity or only for a predetermined number of years
- The rating of the resort
- The available amenities
- Whether the resort is part of a well-known status group of resorts (Marriott, Disney, or Four Seasons, for example)
- The season of the week(s) in question
- The amount of money the resort can get away with charging you

The answer should be in comparison to what you would be spending on vacation accommodations *without* timeshare. For example:

- The average number of nights you pay for hotel/motel accommodations per year
- The average price you pay in today's dollars for those accommodations

> ✔ How many years can you reasonably expect to continue to vacation, barring an unforeseen circumstance like death
>
> ✔ The average rate of hotel/motel inflation per year

Here's an example:

> 7 nights per year
>
> $75 dollars per night
>
> 20 years
>
> 10% inflation per year
>
> $30,071

So, anything less than $30,071 is considered a bargain if it gave you anything more, such as more time, better and more spacious accommodations, more peace of mind, and more on-site amenities.

Ultimately, the question of how much to pay realistically boils down to this: Do you have the money to make regular payments *now* to secure your vacation for the rest of your life?

## *Where should I buy timeshare?*

With almost 6,000 timeshare resorts worldwide, this is a particularly intriguing question. It all depends on what you want to do with your timeshare.

If you want nothing more than to vacation in the same resort every year, then it's a no-brainer: Purchase in that location.

Before you buy in your desired location, however, I advise you to check out at least a handful of resorts there to choose the one you like best, with those amenities and services that most appeal to you. This is the place, after all, where you'll be returning every year for your vacation, and you want to make your best effort to ensure that few surprises or disappointments crop up down the road.

If, however, you prefer to travel to different locations for vacation, purchase in the location that has the most demand, year-round, worldwide, in order to give you the best trading power. If you want to exchange your timeshare week for stays in popular hot-destination areas, it's wise to buy a property that is equally in demand.

Currently, the hottest location is Orlando, Florida, which had more than 52 million visitors in 2004. I think it's safe to say that Orlando is neither the most scenic location in the world nor the most relaxing. It does, however, have a 4-foot-tall mouse, a 7-ton whale, a red-tighted superhero, and seemingly endless top attractions.

According to W. Frank Gilmore, a veteran timeshare sales manager and project director, "the power of your exchange is dependent solely on what you put into the system, not what you take out."

## What is the difference between a fixed week, a floating week, and a points-based system?

Two words: guarantee and flexibility.

- ✓ **Fixed week:** A *fixed week* guarantees your accommodations at the resort for that week and that week only. In most cases, you may exchange your accommodations for a stay in another resort, but keep in mind that your "power" to trade for the destination (and time) you want may be restricted by the type of week you own.

- ✓ **Floating week:** A *floating week* gives you more flexibility, especially in trading, but no guaranteed time at any resort, including your own.

- ✓ **Points-based system:** Many resorts have instituted a *points-based system,* which allows owners to utilize their ownership not only for timeshare stays but also for a variety of travel-related products and services such as hotels, airline tickets, and car rentals.

Be aware that in some cases, points-based ownership is *not* ownership at all. The drawback to most points-based timeshare is that the point values may not be inflation-proof. Although your week of timeshare may be exchanged for a couple of airline tickets this year, next year that same ownership may be good for only one ticket.

## Can I (and/or should I) buy resale?

Of course you can buy resale timeshare, whether from the original owner or a resale company. But keep in mind that it is important to find out why the timeshare is on the resale market. Much of what is out there on the resale market is being sold for what I consider legitimate reasons: death, divorce, underutilization, or need for quick cash. But a good percentage of inexpensive timeshares on the resale market are there because they don't work, or more to the point, don't work as they were promised to work. In other words, cheaper is not always better.

That said, the resale market is hot, and many people have success at the buying-to-trade game. They look for less expensive or up-and-coming destinations to buy — even places they have no intention of visiting — largely for the potential trade value. It's a bit like playing the stock market, and some people do come out as winners.

If you're considering buying timeshare on the resale market, I suggest you hire someone with a legal or timeshare background to do the legwork for you and ensure that it's everything it's advertised to be.

## Resale: One man's tale

I recently met a young man who crowed that, "My daddy bought three weeks of time-share in Galveston, Texas, on the resale market for only $1,000 each" and that, "He won't buy in Orlando because it's too expensive." "Great," I said, "and could you tell me the locations your daddy has been able to exchange for these weeks of time-share?" The young man admitted that actually, his daddy hasn't been able to exchange his Galveston timeshare with any other location so far. "So tell me," I went on, "does your daddy like to vacation in Galveston?" The young man looked at me glumly and shook his head no. "But," he said brightly, "you gotta admit, he got it cheap!"

### *Do I have to go to the same timeshare resort every year?*

No. There are over 5,000 timeshare resorts worldwide. The vast majority of these timeshares belong to either Resort Condominiums International (RCI) or Interval International (II). For a small fee (currently $121–$129), you may trade or exchange your timeshare for comparable accommodations throughout the world.

Timeshare exchange companies operate under certain rules, so just because you own timeshare, you're not guaranteed to be able to trade whenever and wherever you want to go. For more on exchanging, check out Chapter 12.

## *Making Foolish Assumptions*

Because only 3% of people in the United States already own timeshare, it is likely that you're considering buying timeshare for the very first time. If so, be sure to ask all the pertinent questions (see Chapter 7). Even if you've already attended one or more sales presentations, know that each timeshare is different, and you should assume nothing. Be prepared to ask all the pertinent questions wherever you go.

Timeshare sales-presentation veterans keep a list of the answers to their most important questions about each timeshare so that at the end of the day, they can compare and contrast.

Many people start off thinking that timeshare isn't for them because, in their words, "We don't want to go to the same place every year." They assumed that the resort that they were viewing allowed them usage only there, instead of at thousands of resorts worldwide through the beauty of exchanging.

Although the list is endless and varies from customer to customer, here is a list of assumptions that you shouldn't make:

- ✔ All timeshare is deeded forever (they aren't).

- ✔ All timeshare is located in resort areas (they aren't).

- ✔ All damages are always covered by maintenance fees (they aren't).

- ✔ All timeshare units come with a kitchen (some do; some don't).

- ✔ You can let anyone use your timeshare if you're not using it (some resorts have restrictions and/or additional fees).

- ✔ You'll always be able to get what you want in an exchange (you may, depending on where you own and where you want to go).

- ✔ You have to pay to join an exchange company (many resorts pay for this and/or you may not need to join the exchange company).

- ✔ You'll never be able to get what you want in an exchange (you will if you buy at the "right" resort).

- ✔ The maintenance fees will never go up (they may).

- ✔ The maintenance fees always go up (they may not).

- ✔ You can always negotiate the price (maybe you can and maybe you can't; see Chapter 8 for more information).

- ✔ This presentation will be the worst part of your vacation (it doesn't have to be).

The general rule of thumb with timeshares, as with most everything else: The words *never* and *always* are red flags. I always insist that my salesteam avoid using the following four words at any time during the presentation: *free, perfect, always,* and *never*. These concepts don't exist in most of life, and they definitely do not exist in timeshare.

## Use common sense

"You must use common sense with the product. If your salesperson leads you to believe that you can do anything, anytime, think again! If you want to travel during a time of the year that everyone else is, such as a holiday, Mardi Gras, or spring break, don't make your plans a week in advance — nobody else did. This is where common sense comes in. Make your plans accordingly. I know you're thinking, 'Of course, that makes perfect sense! Who would do something that foolish?' and yet I sit down with people every day who wonder why they can't use their timeshare a certain way. And that is because they have unreal expectations about how to use the unit they were sold."

M. Burroughs, Davenport, Florida

Also, don't assume that your salesperson has read this book or is a mind reader. The happiest customers I have — that is, the ones with the most owner satisfaction — continue to be the people who asked questions about what mattered to them, and persisted in doing so even if they assumed they knew the answer.

## Getting More Information

Keep in mind that a timeshare salesperson is but one source of information. You can pursue any number of avenues to get more information about a timeshare resort. Word of mouth is what may have gotten you interested in the first place (and it certainly helps to know people who can provide firsthand experience — and even referrals), but to get the lowdown on what you're getting yourself into, myriad helpful resources are literally at your fingertips. I don't mind tooting my own horn, because I consider my Web site, Timeshare Insights (www.timeshare insights.com), to be an unbiased, independent source of solid consumer information. Check it out, and I hope you find it useful, too.

If your timeshare is affiliated with an exchange company (and it likely is), you can also glean information from the rankings and ratings bestowed by the exchange companies themselves. Both RCI and II award resorts that consistently exceed the company standards of product quality, service delivery, and customer satisfaction. RCI even color codes its resorts by season, from high-demand (red) times to low-demand (blue). Check out the latest RCI (www.rci.com) and II (www.intervalworld.com) catalogs for the latest resort ratings and codes.

You can also find lots of sensible advice and helpful timeshare tips at the following Web sites:

✔ *TimeSharing Today* **magazine** (www.tsdoday.com): In addition to the well-written articles, fair and informational resort reviews, and a wealth of discussion about current issues in the timeshare world, *TimeSharing Today* offers a good listing of timeshare resales and rentals in all areas.

✔ **Timeshare Tips** (www.tstips.com): Timeshare Tips has representatives from four exchange companies online answering questions for their members. In their words, "We recognize that all participants are necessary for a healthy timeshare industry. Although most of our members buy resale, we all recognize that without developer sales, there would be no resales. We also believe that without the ability to resell, developer sales would be more difficult."

✔ **Timeshare Users Group** (www.tug2.net): This online group of timeshare owners posts informational articles and discussions about many subjects (some not even related to timeshares). They also have a growing list of resale timeshares. *Tuggers* as they are called, are a fiercely close, loyal bunch.

✔ ***The Timeshare Beat*** (www.thetimesharebeat.com): *The Beat* is the timeshare industry's most-read publication. The online magazine has many articles about timeshare and a nice section on frauds — this is usually the first place that negative but very necessary information is posted for the public about timeshare in general. *The Timeshare Beat* is free.

# Rating the resorts

"I find the magazine *TimeSharing Today,* along with the Web sites tstoday.com and tug2.net, a wealth of information. You can read reviews from people who have been to resorts. Most of the time, these people are candid in their comments and rate the resort on a scale of 1 to 10. You can also post on the bulletin boards and receive information from other timeshare travelers."

Dianne Loftis, Brentwood, Tennessee

# Part II
# Buying Timeshare

The 5<sup>th</sup> Wave                    By Rich Tennant

"The paperwork for your timeshare seems to be in order. Now, if we can tap a vein for your signature we'll be all set."

## *In this part . . .*

*I* get into the nitty-gritty of buying timeshare. I discuss how timeshare is marketed and sold, what you can expect at a traditional timeshare presentation, and how to handle a sales pitch. I provide you with a list of essential questions to ask before signing on the dotted line and advise on ways to finance your timeshare. I also give the lowdown on the pros and cons of buying resale or through referral programs.

**Chapter 5**

# How Timeshare Is Marketed

*H*ave you ever wondered why you see so few advertisements or television commercials selling timeshare? It's because of the method in which timeshares are marketed and sold. In this chapter, I explain why and how timeshare uses its particular sales model — and why I think it's time to abandon it.

## The Art of the Lure

In the early days of timeshare, when the product was relatively unknown to the public, timeshare resorts started the practice of *gifting* clients to come in and see what they had to offer. You may remember the days when timeshare resorts were routinely giving out toasters, color televisions, dinner certificates, and pretty much the kitchen sink in return for your time listening to a sales presentation.

No one knows exactly why timeshare developers arrived at the idea that their product was too uniquely positioned to take advantage of traditional advertising methods.

With respect to the old-time timeshares, this type of marketing did work to some extent. That is, it filled salesrooms day after day, and some of the people attending the presentations did purchase the product. It also led to the image of the hard-sell timeshare salesperson, the questionable-at-best selling practices so prevalent in the old days, and the often less-than-honest image that timeshare still holds for many consumers. In fact, a recent survey revealed that 79% of consumers polled thought that they had to endure a high-pressure sales presentation in order to purchase a timeshare.

Unfortunately, the timeshare industry is, as a whole, doing little to dissuade consumers from that image — because in truth, the majority of timeshare presentations are the result of some discounted vacation package or other gift.

It would, in my opinion, behoove the industry to wake up and notice that timeshare is no different than any other commercial product out there — and that the timeshare product these days is good enough to easily sell itself without having to lure customers to presentations with offers of free vacations or gifts. Compare the advertising and marketing efforts of the following:

**Product A:** The advertising agency or the advertising department of Product A has done its research and found that the target audience of this product is as follows:

- Is a member of a family of four consisting of two adults (ages 38–57) and two children (ages 5–17)

- Has a household income of $50,000+

- Is a homeowner

- Has traveled at least three times in the past five years

- Regularly subscribes to at least one travel magazine

For a fee of $13,000, the ad agency now prepares an advertising plan consisting of:

- Half-page color advertisements in the top three travel magazines

- Thirty-second radio spots in the top ten markets in the country targeting adults 39–54

- Half-page advertisements in the Sunday newspaper once per month in the top ten markets in the country

The ads consist of photos of the "typical happy family" using Product A, some basic information about Product A, a snappy headline to draw the reader's attention — and, of course, the name, address, and phone number of the local retail establishment where Product A can be purchased. It's simple, basic, tried and true, and designed to get people thinking about Product A, look at Product A at a local retailer, and purchase Product A.

Now compare this with how timeshares advertise their product with similar target demographics:

**Product B:** The timeshare will pay a marketing company upward of $350 to get a body in the door in order to sell Product B. A typical busy day in Orlando, Myrtle Beach, Gatlinburg, or Las Vegas brings in 100 customers, which costs the timeshare $35,000.

Timeshares are paying marketing companies to sell vacation packages to anyone, regardless of ability to purchase, tendency to purchase, or interest in purchasing.

The makers of Product A are paying their advertising agency to get people to look at and ultimately purchase the product in question, not see or do something else.

And what's the difference in the customers? The people who saw the ads and heard the radio spots for Product A visit the retailer because they're interested in the product being advertised. They may or may not buy it,

## Shedding a shady reputation

In the early days of timeshare, particularly in Florida, parts of Pennsylvania, California, and Nevada, the timeshare industry used as it primary selling tool the practice of luring potential buyers with vacation offers, wining and dining, and the opportunity to buy shares in lovely resorts "soon to be built." They promised luxury gifts that turned out to be duds, and offered free vacation prizes that were anything but free — all to get consumers to attend 90-minute sales presentations that often turned into daylong marathons of hard selling. In the worst-case scenarios, as soon as the contract was signed, the salesperson and the "developer" absconded with the money, leaving the consumer with shoddy or third-rate property that had little in common with the land touted at the sales presentations — or even worse, a deed to nothing.

Part of the problem was the timeshare hawkers' propensity to play bait-and-switch games — dangling the words "free vacation" and "no obligation" to draw people to hard-sell timeshare presentations. They found creative ways to prey on hapless customers looking for a little piece of paradise by promising luxury gifts, developing Byzantine contracts, using opaque language — even pushing emotional blackmail ("after all these years, don't you think your wife deserves a reward?") on a captive audience.

As a result, some people made a lot of money. Some people were satisfied with their purchases, but too many others got burned. The perception, fair or not, of a heartless sales force selling mediocre product to innocent consumers began to sully the entire industry.

The timeshare community knew that it was in its own best interests to shed its shady image. The most egregious of the violators were run out of town. States passed laws regulating timeshares, and the industry itself adopted provisions to weed out scam artists and provide a template and a model code for developers and marketers alike.

Timeshare developers in Europe, where it all began nearly 50 years ago, are also cleaning up their act. *The Wall Street Journal's RealEstate Journal* reported that regulations in Europe are forcing timeshare developers to follow stricter standards of practice. For example, in Europe, contracts are required to be written not only in the language of the country where the timeshare is located, but in the native language of the buyer as well.

but they are motivated enough to investigate the product. The people at the timeshare resort are there because they paid for and received an inexpensive vacation, not because they're interested in the product, in this case timeshare.

The salesperson at the retail store will have an easier time selling the product simply because the consumer has shown initiative in pursuing the product. The timeshare salesperson has a much harder time, merely because his customers aren't really interested in the product — they're interested in a cheap vacation, which is what they signed on for. It's no wonder that with more than 3.5 million Americans attending timeshare presentations each year, after some 30 years, only 6.5 million families own timeshare. The marketing companies have been hired to sell vacation packages, not timeshare.

But wait, you may say: Isn't the fact that they are on vacation at a timeshare resort indicative of their interest in buying a timeshare? Not necessarily. The key difference is that the timeshare customer has paid his or her money for a vacation and is now being forced to listen to a timeshare pitch. The customer in the retail establishment hasn't paid a dime and isn't being forced to listen to anything. No wonder timeshare has a reputation for the hard sell. To me, it's completely unnecessary because most timeshare product on the market today is quality enough to sell without this sort of gimmickry.

## Marketing Companies and Their Tactics

The vast majority of consumers are solicited to attend a timeshare presentation via a vacation offer. You've probably received something like this in the mail:

"Congratulations, <u>your name</u>, you are the official recipient of four fabulous days and three nights in beautiful and sunny Orlando, Florida! Your wonderful vacation also includes:

- ✔ Three days and two nights in beautiful Fort Lauderdale
- ✔ Seven days transportation by <u>name of car rental company</u>

And <u>your name</u>, if you call within the next 48 hours, you will also receive:

- ✔ Four days and three nights in exciting Las Vegas
- ✔ Four days and three nights in fun-filled Gatlinburg

Call toll-free 1-800-xxx-xxxx between the hours of 8:00 a.m. and 7:00 p.m., Monday through Friday, to claim your exciting vacation package. Due to the overwhelming response to this fabulous package, you are limited to one call per package please."

Sometimes these packages have a very low price attached to them or you may receive a voucher to cover the cost of the vacations. You may be told that you'll stay at a brand-name hotel (or the equivalent); sometimes the package will include photos of well-known sights at the destination.

And inevitably, somewhere on the solicitation, usually in 8-point type-face, you will see something like, "THIS ADVERTISING MATERIAL IS BEING USED FOR THE PURPOSE OF SOLICITING SALES OF A VACATION OWNERSHIP PLAN." (The words *timeshare* and *vacation ownership* are interchangeable.)

## Marketing timeshare by phone, fax, and e-mail

Marketing companies have also routinely used phone calls, faxes, and e-mail to attempt to snag clients for the timeshare presentation.

With the passage of the no-call legislation back in 2003, many timeshare marketing companies were forced to look for alternative ways of market-ing. Unfortunately, they still haven't yet gone the traditional route, resorting instead to offering these same types of packages via fax machine. No-fax legislation, scheduled to go into effect in 2005, again is going to leave marketing companies scrambling for another way to market these packages.

If you receive one of these offers, realize that 99.9% of the time, you will be required to take one or more timeshare presentations, even if the telemarketer tells you that you won't.

This type of timeshare "marketing" serves only to undermine the indus-try and leads to the question, "If I'm being bribed, is there something wrong with the product?"

Here are some questions to ask when you are talking with a timeshare telemarketer. (Keep in mind that most telemarketing calls are monitored or recorded, a practice that is usually mandated by state laws.)

- ✔ Does this package require a timeshare or vacation ownership presentation?
- ✔ Which timeshares or resorts will I be required to visit?
- ✔ Does this package come with a rental car? If not, how will I get to the resort or timeshare?
- ✔ What are all the costs of this package? Does this price include all taxes? Are there surcharges?
- ✔ Is there a local number I can call if something goes wrong once I get there?
- ✔ What are the cancellation penalties?

# They just won't take no for an answer

Sometimes you have to be firm with telephone marketers. After I had signed up for the federal do-not-call list, I received a call from a marketer for a timeshare located just two minutes from my house. I was invited to "enjoy a complimentary one-hour visit of our beautiful resort with no obligation to purchase anything, but your family will receive two tickets to one of central Florida's world-famous attractions." I first informed the caller that I was single and didn't have a family. The invitation was still good, I was told. I then politely informed the caller that I sold timeshare at another resort and simply wasn't interested. The invitation was cheerfully repeated, and I was told that "you are under no obligation to purchase anything." Finally, I told the gentleman that I was on the do-not-call list and that this call was in violation of the law. After a pause on the other end, he chirped, "Well, if you change your mind, this offer is valid for the next six months!" I hung up and reported the call.

If you don't want to be solicited for these types of promotional travel packages, it is your responsibility to sign up for *No Call* and *No Fax* lists. Consumers can easily do this by registering their phone number at www.donotcall.gov or calling the toll-free number (☎ 888-382-1222). If the marketing companies reach you on your phone or fax after you've registered, inform them that you are on this list and that if you're contacted again, you will report the violation.

## Getting wise to OPCs

Another marketing tactic still in rampant use among timeshare resorts is the ubiquitous *off-property consultants* (OPCs). What are OPCs? In Orlando, OPCs operate ticket/information booths scattered amid the high-traffic tourist centers. In Las Vegas, OPCs are everywhere up and down the Strip. In Mexico, OPCs come up to you on the beach and entice you with discounted tickets or free dinners just for viewing their resort.

With telemarketing calls, you generally have the protection of the entire conversation being recorded, which gives you something to fall back on, if necessary. With OPCs, that protection has been taken away from you. Sometimes, the offers and discounts you receive from OPCs are legitimate — and sometimes they're scams. Often, the OPC is simply being paid to bring bodies into timeshare resorts, regardless of a person's ability or interest in the product. In this instance, who is being scammed? Unfortunately, both the consumer *and* the timeshare resort.

Use this as your mantra: If it sounds too good to be true, it often is. Go with your gut feeling. Does the OPC look reputable? Did he or she answer your questions? Do you think the tickets or dinner coupons look legitimate?

## Scam alert: Little white lies

Off-property consultants (OPCs) will convince unwitting tourists to lie about the amount of money they earn, their employment status, and/or their marital status (sometimes going as far as giving unmarried friends fake wedding bands) in order to get paid for delivering bodies to the resort. The resort and the salesperson now have to spend valuable time with these clients, when everyone involved knows that a sale is virtually impossible.

 Not all OPCs are evil scam artists. Starwood has a very lovely OPC desk right in the lobby of the luxurious Atlantis Resort in the Bahamas. If you stop in, as I did, you may be offered two free dinners at a fine restaurant in exchange for viewing the Starwood Vacation Ownership property, Harborside, adjacent to the Atlantis Resort. I signed up, took a presentation that lasted about 105 minutes, didn't buy, didn't get pressured to buy, and received my dinner vouchers. Everything was as promised.

## The Biggest Secret about Timeshare That Developers Don't Want You to Know

In a recent survey, more than 79% of people surveyed thought that it was necessary to sit through a high-pressure sales presentation in order to purchase a timeshare.

Many consumers find themselves at a timeshare after purchasing some sort of vacation package or obtaining discount attraction tickets or other gifts. In those cases, it *is* necessary to sit through the timeshare presentation given by the resort and the salesperson.

If, however, after reading this book you decide to visit a timeshare or two on your own and gather some information on-site, you are under no obligation to sit through a presentation. Although timeshares have always hired marketing companies to go out there and snatch bodies for them to tour, that doesn't mean that's the only way to gather information about the resort. You, the informed consumer, can go into any timeshare in the world, ask to speak with someone in sales, and inquire about viewing a model and getting price quotes. In these instances, you do not have to sit through any sales presentation to buy a timeshare unit. This is a fact that the resort and marketing companies prefer to keep under wraps.

Timeshare is a product for sale to the consumer. If you go into an auto dealer, are you required to sit through a 90-minute presentation on the virtues of their latest model? Of course not. You are free to come in, see the model, ask for the price, and decide whether you want to buy.

The timeshare industry and the timeshare marketing companies have convinced themselves that you, the consumer, are not able to make the decision to purchase timeshare on your own unless you sit through a two-hour (and sometimes half-day) sales pitch.

If you do decide to take an independent look at a timeshare resort, know that you may be mildly coerced into attending a sales presentation. You are under no obligation to do so. If you're not allowed to simply walk into a resort and get basic information and prices, that should tell you something — perhaps that you should stay away.

And, if, after you're shown the property (don't expect to walk around by yourself, resorts are usually restricted to owners only, and that's a good thing), you ask the price, be prepared: More games may follow. Most timeshare operators offer consumers a discount for buying today. If you've walked in without being required to sit through a sales pitch and aren't prepared to buy on the spot, politely tell the salesperson or tour guide that you understand about the discount, but you will not be purchasing today and would like the price anyway.

Again, my advice to you is simple: If you aren't given a price, just walk away and don't do business with them.

Many timeshares are available on the resale market, and the advantage of this is that you bypass the sales pitch, which may or may not be high pressure. Of course, resale has its own set of issues, which are addressed in more detail in Chapter 9.

Although the majority of salespersons out there, timeshare or other, are decent, hard-working, honest people, it is their goal to sell you their product, not the competition's. If you walk into a Ford dealership, the salesperson is going to try to persuade you to buy a Ford, not a Chevy.

The most informative (and fairly pressure-free) way I know of buying timeshare is to hire a *timeshare consultant* who merely consults and doesn't actually sell anything other than expertise. This way, no bias is shown and no one timeshare or timeshare system is pushed.

# Chapter 6

# The Timeshare Sales Presentation

As a timeshare salesperson and consultant, I have conducted many timeshare sales presentations. When done professionally and considerately, these sales presentations are entertaining, offer a positive and productive give-and-take, and leave the participants feeling that it was time well spent.

But the timeshare sales pitch has retained a somewhat negative image from the days when the industry was something of an unregulated Wild West. The image of flim-flamming salespeople furiously peddling a questionable product is one that refuses to fade away. And for good reason: The hard sell is still around in various permutations. In this chapter, you discover how some salespeople are trained to keep you in a highly emotional state — and more importantly, how you can avoid being controlled by a salesperson by becoming an informed consumer and asking the right questions.

## Before You Go

So you're signed up for a timeshare sales presentation. My first recommendation? Bring a copy of *Timeshare Vacations For Dummies*, 1st Edition, with you when you go. Savvy salespeople appreciate the fact that you've done your homework. (If they're *really* savvy, they'll have read the book themselves!)

---

## It's a fact: Sales presentation statistics

The timeshare industry is a $5.5 billion industry, and sales presentations are a key part of the selling machine. It's estimated that approximately three million people attend timeshare sales presentations a year. Of these, 10% of the attendees end up buying timeshare.

---

Now, I'm not asking or expecting you to just walk in, sit down in front of the salesperson, shake his or her hand, hand over your credit card and say "I'd like to buy a two-bedroom timeshare." I am asking you to go into this experience with an open mind, ask the right questions (see Chapter 7) and decide for yourself whether the product makes sense for you.

## *The Sales Presentation: What to Expect*

In this section, I lay out the basic elements of the timeshare sales presentation, from start to finish.

 Almost all timeshare presentations have been prearranged for a specific date and a specific time. Most are scheduled for a minimum of 90 minutes. This means that in order to receive any gifts (attraction tickets, dinner vouchers, cash) or discounted or free hotel stays that were part of whatever package or deal got you there in the first place, you must complete the tour or presentation.

Although they vary from resort to resort, from brand name to brand name, and from salesperson to salesperson, sales presentations follow the same general outline. Some resorts have their salespersons conduct the entire presentation in one place, while others move to different locations.

### *Greeting*

During this phase of the sales presentation, the salesperson is merely saying hello and making introductions. It's get-to-know-you time, where the salesperson may ask questions like: "Where are you from?" "Is this your first time in this area?" and "Did you have any problems finding the resort?"

### *Warm-up*

Although you should never underestimate the entertainment factor in a timeshare presentation, don't expect a song-and-dance extravaganza. In getting the audience primed for the rest of the show, a salesperson makes small talk and gets to know the participants better. A good salesperson makes an effort to put everyone at ease — *not* to intimidate them.

# The sales presentation: Your role

Here's a checklist of your role in the sales presentation:

☑ Get there on time.

☑ Do your homework before you arrive.

☑ Be wary of a company or person that uses the words *free, perfect, always,* or *never* in materials or speech.

☑ If you aren't comfortable with your salesperson, it's absolutely fine to request another.

☑ Don't drink alcohol before or during the presentation.

☑ Always check the salesperson's math.

## Intent statement

This is where the salesperson gets down to business and discusses why he or she is here and what you can expect of the next 90 or so minutes.

## Discovery

A discovery is just that: a way for the salesperson to discover more about you, the way you vacation, what you like to do on vacation, why you vacation, how much money you spend on vacation, and where you would like to go on vacation. The salesperson will likely ask you what types of problems you have encountered on vacations and what could make your vacations better.

 Contrary to popular belief, during the discovery period, timeshare salespersons are not asking trick questions, nor are there specific questions or answers that mark or identify buyers and nonbuyers.

## Replay

After the salesperson has completed asking questions, he or she will generally replay the information back to you, in order to make sure that what you said is what the salesperson heard and to make the rest of the presentation interesting to you.

## Company credibility

If you're taking a timeshare presentation at a name-brand resort, a Hilton or Marriott, for example, you will generally be shown pictures, testimonials, posters, or even roomfuls of company information. If you are at a nonbrand timeshare, the salesperson will generally tell you something about the resort, the managing company, and the builders. Here are some real-life examples of the variety of sales tools you may encounter:

## Are you hungry yet?

Most timeshare resorts offer their clients some sort of food. This ranges from bran muffins, bagels, bananas, and coffee, to a full breakfast or lunch, sometimes miles away from where you and your salesperson meet.

- 3-D topographic maps of the property
- Huge light-up maps showing all the resort locations
- Movies
- Newspaper or magazine clippings with quotes about the company or about timeshare in general

### Financial logic/solution

The financial logic is the basis on which most standard timeshare is sold. Some salespeople write on a simple piece of blank paper; others use preprinted forms. A few name-brand resorts have high-tech flat-screen computers into which the salespersons enter data. One resort uses a hands-on approach: having the clients enter their own data on a large touch pad, the results of which they then show on a 52-inch screen.

### Product options

This, along with the property or model tour that follows, is generally the part of the presentation that clients find the most fun.

This may be the first time that the RCI or II Directory of Resorts is shown to you. Some resorts have elaborate rooms or hallways full of photos of resorts. Many resorts use a film or slide show to show the various locations you can exchange with your timeshare and the activities you and your family can enjoy.

This is also the time that the salesperson will explain the type of timeshare being offered (fixed week, floating week, points, and so on) and how you can use what you own. For more on the specific types of timeshare, see Chapter 3.

### Model tour

Whether you walk, take a golf cart, drive in your car, ride in the salesperson's car, take a boat ride, or load into a van or bus, at some point you will leave the location to actually see the property and/or the model.

At this time and during the closing (see the following section), ask your first-tier and second-tier questions (see Chapter 7).

## And here's Petey Jr. . . .

For reasons I have yet to understand, many salespeople insist on showing pictures of themselves and their family on vacation. Although the goal is to give you something dynamic to look at, instead of showing pictures in a directory, I'm not sure it does any good other than inflate the ego of the salesperson.

### Closing

You either return to where you started from or move to another area where the salesperson or sales manager asks you whether you have any questions. They then begin the *closing,* or sales process. (For more information, see Chapter 8.)

## Buying Timeshare Today . . . Or Not

For many people, the most perplexing, misunderstood, and suspicious issue about buying timeshare at a sales presentation is the issue of buying today, on the spot, after spending only two hours with a salesperson.

Understand that the salesperson has a job to do. Further understand that as a salesperson, his or her aim is to sell you a timeshare that day. And make no mistake about it; you will be asked to buy today, generally at the end of the sales presentation.

This may sound like a paradox, but it's really not: In the selling of most timeshare, it is the salesperson's job to get you to sign today — but it is not the salesperson's job to force a customer into buying anything they don't want or can't afford. That's just unethical and bad business to boot. Customer satisfaction with a product is what drives any business — and if you're reduced to forcing people to buy something with threats or ultimatums, that's an indication that the product is a lemon.

Case in point: Although the buy-today philosophy is standard practice at most resorts around the world, it is far less prevalent with higher-end products, such as fractionals and private residence clubs (see Chapter 16). Interestingly enough, the Disney Vacation Club (among others) does not adhere to a strict "buy-today" policy — and has profited from it. Since its beginnings 14 years ago, Disney Vacation Club members now total more than 80,000.

## Let the client buy

"Our product has changed so much in the past 20 years. In 1980, the client was essentially buying one week per year in the Poconos or Myrtle Beach. And they were on their own from there. Today, we sell one of the most attractive leisure products in the world — evidenced by double-digit growth, hotel-brand awareness, and Wall Street attention. But we don't need to sell the product the way we did 20 years ago. Sometimes we try so hard to sell that we don't allow people to buy. I have heard execs in the past year still preaching the merits of high-pressure sales, but I don't want to know their cancellation rates. Give a presentation that highlights the value of ownership so well that the client is asking you to let them buy. This is not timeshare Utopia; it is a real place, and you can be a resident."

Michael S. Finn, Registered Resort Professional (RRP)

## *Why today?*

Why do timeshares insist on having you do business right there on the spot? And should you buy right there on the spot? What are your alternatives? What happens if you don't buy on the spot? Can you buy the next day at the same price? Is it legal for timeshares to raise the price tomorrow? What happens if you call their bluff?

To clear up some of the confusion, I start with three simple facts:

- ✔ You are under no obligation to purchase any timeshare from anyone, at any time, today or tomorrow.

- ✔ The developer, like any good businessperson, is in business to sell the product today rather than later.

- ✔ Despite what developers and consumers seem to think, timeshare is like any other product, subject to supply, demand, and marketing costs.

Before I look at the today issue as it pertains to timeshare, consider any other consumer product — a men's suit, for example. There you are, sitting at home on a Sunday morning, leisurely reading the paper. You see a full-page ad from your local retailer featuring a full-color photo of a dashing young man in a crisply tailored suit. The headline reads:

One-Day Sale! All Suits Slashed 25% Off!

"Hmmm," you think to yourself, "I don't *really* need a new suit, but the old one is a bit dated, and 25% off is a good savings."

You have three options at this point:

- ✔ Get up off the couch that day, get dressed, go to the mall, find the store, try on a suit or two, buy one or even two and save 25%.

- ✔ Don't get up off the couch until Tuesday, get dressed, go the mall, find the store, try on a suit or two, buy one or two and pay full price.

- ✔ Don't get up off the couch at all, and don't buy any suits, regardless of the price.

Do you believe the store is being unfair, pushy, demanding, or, worse yet, illegal by insisting that you pay full price for the suit on Tuesday that you could have gotten for 25% off on Sunday? I doubt it. Almost all products are advertised and marketed that way. Car manufacturers and dealers do it all the time.

When timeshare salespersons offer you an incentive to do business today, it's because that's what they are in business to do . . . make the sale today.

## The vacation factor

Like any other vacation property, timeshares are not a necessity. You can live your entire life quite well without a timeshare. To me, however, vacations are a necessity. And whenever I fall in love with a vacation destination, I start looking at local real estate ads and dreaming of having a piece of property there to come back to year after year. Apparently, I'm not alone. And no one understands this phenomenon better than realtors and timeshare developers.

It also explains why the vast majority of people who do eventually buy a timeshare make the purchase while they're on vacation. It makes sense: You're away from your everyday stresses; you're relaxing and enjoying the beauty of the place. If you could only find a reasonable way to come back here every year to recharge your batteries. . . .

This is where timeshare and timeshare sales presentations come in. What better place to introduce the possibility of ownership in a destination than when the potential client is falling in love with it! Because by the time you come home from a vacation, it's back to reality. You're unpacking, doing laundry, checking the mail, paying bills, going back to work. The last thing on your mind is the timeshare you saw a week ago.

## You like it, but . . .

So, you're interested in a timeshare but you don't have full confidence that this particular timeshare is right for you. What do you do?

- ✔ To clear your head, ask your salesperson to leave you alone for a bit, or if possible, ask to leave the sales area for some quiet time.

✔ I often advise clients to go with their gut feeling. What is your honest feeling about what you have been shown? Do you have concerns about using the timeshare properly? Is the price of the product an issue? Was the salesperson unclear about anything? Did something just not add up?

✔ If you're still undecided, discuss whether the discount offers or other perks for buying right there on the spot can be extended. If the salesperson flat-out refuses to discuss options with you, again, my recommendation is to go with your gut feeling.

✔ Ask whether it's possible to leave a 100% refundable deposit on the timeshare for a day or two to get your own feelings sorted out.

Be realistic. You're dealing with real estate here. Unlike traditional retail establishments, both buyers and sellers are held to a somewhat higher standard. You wouldn't ask a home developer to simply hold a house for you without some sort of deposit or earnest money, would you?

## Sales presentation veterans

"Having owned a timeshare since the early 1980s, we've attended our share of timeshare presentations. Lately, we've noticed that the presentations have gotten a bit easier on the hard-sell portion. I think it's in reaction to the bad publicity a few rotten apples have given the whole industry.

One facility we looked at is on the points system, which wasn't appealing to us and we told them so. That didn't dampen the salesperson's enthusiasm a bit. He proceeded on with his pitch for 10,000 points for $29,999. He offered a five-year payment plan, after 20% down, for only 18.9% annual interest. I expressed shock at that figure, but the agent just brushed it aside, saying, "That's what they're getting these days." Not from me, fella!

After hearing about their facilities around the world, we let the salesperson know that we were completely happy with our two weeks in Hawaii, and would not be buying today. At this point, he called in his manager, who presented two more alternatives; one 5,000-point package and another 3,000-point package at somewhat reduced prices. Plus, he threw in the requisite one-day only incentives and other minor perks designed to get you to sign up today. After we convinced the manager that we weren't ready to buy, another manager came by and proceeded to present one last option: a 10,000-point deal good for 18 months for only $1,500 and an additional discount to $1,325 — again, if we sign up today. When we politely declined that offer, that was the end of the sell. The manager made out our gift certificate. Everyone was very cordial and polite, and we really didn't feel a great deal of pressure."

Gordon P. Cress, Carlsbad, California

For some people, shopping around at a few timeshares is worth the loss of the first-day incentive or added perks. It's perfectly fine to do so — and don't ever let the salesperson make you feel bad if you do. Ultimately, it is your money and your choice.

## *Handling the Sales Pitch*

The truth about most timeshare sales presentations: They last a *minimum* of 90 minutes. Snacks and drinks may or may not be served. Vouchers or gifts (the incentives that got you in there in the first place) are given away last.

You may be surprised to know that although almost no one comes into a sales presentation with buying timeshare in mind, about one in four people do buy. Keeping an open mind doesn't mean you have to buy anything. Keeping an open mind merely means when the time comes to purchase or not, you can make an intelligent, informed choice.

I'm astonished at the number of clients, buyers and nonbuyers alike, who ask almost no questions throughout the presentation, and then make a decision at the end. Sometimes, clients feel that it is up to the

## They've heard it all

Much of timeshare sales training consists of ways to address (translate: overcome) customer objections. Here are some of the most commonly heard objections from potential buyers. Know that your salesperson has been trained to come up with a snappy retort to:

✔ We need to think about it.

✔ We can't make a decision today.

✔ We made a vow not to make hasty decisions.

✔ We aren't looking for another bill to pay.

✔ We need to talk to our attorney.

✔ We don't like paying maintenance fees.

✔ We would rather invest our money than spend it on a timeshare.

✔ The resort sure is making a lot of money.

✔ We only sleep in our room; we don't need more than a bed.

✔ We're campers.

✔ We have to consult our (children, parents, accountant, astrologer).

salesperson to tell them everything. That is dangerous. Sometimes, clients just don't know what questions to ask. To help you, I provide both first-tier (the most important) and second-tier (less important but still invaluable) questions in Chapter 7.

I advise people to come to a sales presentation with a list of questions that need answered. You have a right to expect direct answers to your questions. If you don't, you're probably with the wrong salesperson.

 If you're traveling with children under the age of 2, try to leave them at home. Babies are adorable but a distraction for both you and the salesperson. And, if you have a tough time getting up early on vacation, don't schedule your presentation for 8 a.m.

One last pet peeve: A great number of people out there attend numerous timeshare presentations each year — or worse still, each day of their vacation — knowing perfectly well that they have no intention of buying timeshare, today or any day. They're just in it for the freebies or vacation vouchers. I realize that the industry has allowed this to happen, but it's a bit of a reverse scam — and, frankly, a waste of everyone's time.

## *Oops! What Was 1 Thinking?*

Suppose you buy today and wake up tomorrow regretting you did. You're in luck: Depending on the jurisdiction that the timeshare must adhere to, you may be legally entitled to a cancellation or cooling-off period called a *rescission period*. The rescission clause states that you're legally entitled to all your money back (full or down payment) if you change your mind.

Some countries like St. Martin have no rescission period: You buy it; you own it. In Florida, state law gives consumers 10 days for rescission. Most of Europe also has 10 days, with the exception of the United Kingdom, which generally offers 14 days.

 A rescission period is *not* meant to be used to hop from timeshare to timeshare, leaving a deposit here and there and then coming back and asking for your money back. The rescission clause was put in to protect consumers, not penalize timeshare resorts.

# Chapter 7

# You're Interested: Asking the Right Questions

*In This Chapter*

▶ Getting answers to the primary questions
▶ Getting answers to the secondary questions

ou've taken a tour of the timeshare facilities, and your interest is definitely high. Now is the time to ask those essential questions that will help you make your final decision. This chapter gives you the lowdown on which questions to ask and the answers to look for.

## The First-Tier Questions

These are the deal-breaker questions, the ones any responsible timeshare salesperson should readily have the answers to. It's always a good idea to take notes as you go along — and, if you decide to buy, ask that everything be spelled out in the contract.

### Is the timeshare a deeded ownership, a right-to-use system, or a points-based system?

If you're looking for the best type of timeshare here, there simply isn't one. Your choice of timeshare depends on what you want to do with it, how much control you want, and how long you and/or your heirs plan on using the timeshare. To help you decide, I give you the following descriptions of each system.

#### Deeded ownerships

In most cases in the United States, deeded property is deeded in perpetuity, which means it is willable as well as sellable. Always ask, though. And ask whether you as the owner have the right to rent your usage if you can't vacation one year. You should always purchase the timeshare that gives you the very most in flexibility and control.

### Right-to-use system

A right-to-use property generally indicates that the property has X number of uses. That use number could be 20 or 100; it could mean one use per year for 20 years or 20 uses, period. If, for example, you buy 20 uses and go on ten vacations a year, in two years, you're finished. Right-to-use can also expire in a certain year. Some resorts promise a right-to-extend, although know that no resort is going to just give you more uses without charging you for them.

### Points-based system

Many timeshare resorts and many timeshare companies operate on points-based systems. With a points-based system, you aren't actually buying a timeshare, you're buying an interest in a resort or in an exchange company. The biggest plus for a points-based system is that it generally offers more flexibility.

The biggest minus (and it's a *big* one) is that many times the points are *not* inflation proof, which in my opinion is one of the major reasons for purchasing a timeshare in the first place: to have a hedge against future vacation costs. Again, always ask whether or not the points are inflation proof.

## If the timeshare is deeded, is it transferable?

It's important to know whether your property can be willed, sold, rented, or loaned. Look for a yes on each of these questions.

## If the timeshare is a points-based system, can the points change?

One of the major reasons for purchasing a timeshare is to offset future vacation inflation — whether this inflation is estimated in dollars or points. My advice: If the points needed to make a transaction can increase, make sure to ask whether the value of what you own will also increase. If the answer is no, I say stay clear.

## Is the timeshare a fixed week or a floating week?

Most deeded timeshare is sold in either a fixed-week or a floating-week system. Most points-based timeshare is, by default, floating.

### Fixed week

A *fixed week* is just that; you have the same week of the year available every year. There are two main benefits to a fixed week:

- ✔ If you know you'll be going to your home resort the same week of the year, your timeshare will be waiting for you, no reservations necessary.

✔ If you own an extremely high-demand fixed week (Race Week in Daytona, Florida, for example, or Carnivale Week in Venice, Italy), you will have maximum trading power. Although you still need to make reservations if you wish to exchange, you're putting an extremely desirable week into the trading pool of available weeks — and you will likely be rewarded with a top-demand trade.

 There is a misconception that a fixed week of timeshare means that you must go on vacation the same week every single year. In most cases, that is not true. A fixed week simply means that the resort puts your specific week into the trading pool every year if you choose not to use it.

 Whether you're talking about a fixed week or a floating week, unless you're speaking about points-based timeshare, location is the most important criterion for determining trading power. An October week in Orlando, Florida, will still out-trade a Christmas week in West Virginia, simply because the demand for the latter is much lower.

### Floating week

Ownership in a *floating week* gives you access to a week of the year, but you need to reserve a specific time each year — and the sooner, the better. The floating week option is good if you're concerned about unforeseen work or scheduling conflicts associated with a fixed week. A floating week also gives you more opportunity to travel during your requested time frame.

 A floating week is, more often than not, a floating week within a specific season of the year.

Timeshare resorts have come up with names for the different seasons (for example, Diamond, Ruby, and Sapphire; Adventure, Leisure, and Value; or High and Low), and color codes designating the trading power of your timeshare. It's no wonder that trading can get downright complicated. Consider the following example:

Tim and Nancy go on vacation with Roger and Janice to Orlando, Florida. They both decide to purchase a week of timeshare at the same resort. Both couples purchase in the Diamond (high) season, and both couples pay the same amount for their timeshare. In essence, the couples have identical trading power.

The following year, Tim and Nancy want to trade their timeshare week for a week in Kona, Hawaii, in March while Roger and Janice want to go to Bali, Indonesia, for a week in April. Tim and Nancy make their request a month before Roger and Jane make theirs. The resort thus has to put a week of timeshare into the trading pool for both couples. Although each of the couples own in the same season, Tim and Nancy's week has more trading power.

Because the timeshares they own are in high-demand Orlando, both of these couples are able to make solid high-season exchanges. But timing (when the week is deposited into the system) and home resort location are far more important to the overall trading picture than the very small difference between weeks in a hot location like Orlando.

The problem with a floating week is that because the resort is in charge of depositing "a" week rather than "the" week, your power can change from year to year — it's really about availability and timing — and, of course, location.

## Why buy at this particular resort?

With more than 6,000 timeshare resorts available worldwide, it's important to understand what your timeshare will get you. You'll either use your timeshare at your home resort or exchange it for other resorts. If you wish to go to the same area, state, attraction, or country often (say, seven out of ten years), purchase at the resort in that area you like best, at the place that offers the most amenities, and at the one that is the most affordable for you. If you prefer to visit different areas, states, attractions, or countries (say, seven out of ten years), purchase in a high-demand area, such as Orlando, Las Vegas, or Tenerife. If you buy timeshare in Arkansas, Alabama, or Albania, you'll have a tough time trading your timeshare, simply because these destinations are less in demand.

Note the old adage: The power of your exchange depends solely on what you put into the timeshare system, not what you take out. Cheap timeshare is more often than not just cheap timeshare. Don't sacrifice quality or trading power just to get the least expensive product out there.

You can find out a lot about a resort through the industry's own rankings and ratings system. Both RCI and II, the best-known exchange companies (see Chapter 12), award resorts that consistently exceed the company standards of product quality, service delivery, and customer satisfaction. The top designation for RCI resorts is the RCI Gold Crown; for II it's Five-Star. These awards are deemed the highest level of excellence in resort accommodations and hospitality.

## What are the maintenance fees?

Maintenance fees (and sometimes real estate taxes) are a part of timeshare life. You have to pay them, and pay them every year even after your timeshare deed is paid off. There is no such thing as free maintenance fees, although sometimes the resort pays the fees the first year as an incentive for you to purchase.

Ask what the maintenance fees are, what they cover, and how much they go up annually — and get it in writing. Generally, maintenance fees should cover normal wear and tear, property insurance, liability insurance, utilities (water, gas, electric, phone, cable), and repair and upkeep. Many resorts located on a golf course or on the water also charge special assessments to cover the cost of a system overhaul or repair.

# Timesharing with pets

Can't bear the thought of leaving Zephyr the Wonder Dog behind while you explore the French countryside? Does Sasha the cat look forlorn as you pack your beach accessories for Florida? Both RCI and II offer timeshare resorts that have designated pet-friendly units. Here are a few things you should know about pet-friendly timeshare resorts:

✔ Many of the resorts that do accept pets tend to change their policies on a moment's notice. It's wise to call the resort *immediately* before you make a reservation to see what the pet policy is and what fees, if any, are imposed.

✔ Although most resorts don't accept pets (except for assistance dogs who travel with people with disabilities), many have arrangements with local kennels to board animals during your vacation week.

✔ In general, European timeshares are more pet-friendly than American timeshares ... Fifi the French poodle is much more traveled than your Bowser!

✔ A recent search on the II Web site found 101 pet-friendly resorts; France leads the pack with 13 pet-friendly resorts, while Florida ranks number-one in the United States with 11.

## How much did the maintenance fees go up last year?

In addition to finding out what the maintenance fees are, also ask (because no one will offer this information) whether they have gone up during the preceding two or three years. Never, I repeat *never*, buy from a salesperson who tells you that the maintenance fees never go up. If the maintenance fees aren't going up every now and then, what is happening to the value of your property? It's going down, and that's a bad sign. Ask, too, whether the resort has a cap on any maintenance-fee increase. If you don't get a clear-cut answer to these questions, don't buy from that resort.

## Who votes on what happens with the maintenance fees?

In many resorts, a *homeowners' association (HOA)* is in charge of running the daily operations of the resort (outside of the sales department), including voting on and allocating the maintenance fees. In the best-case scenarios, resorts let the owners have a say in the amount and allocation of information. You're looking for places that give you, the owner, the most control.

## Is the salesperson you're dealing with licensed by the state or country?

Although having a real estate license in no way means someone is a better or more honest salesperson than someone who doesn't, I strongly recommend that if you're buying deeded real estate, you work with a salesperson who is licensed to sell timeshare.

Here's why: Not all states require a real estate license, which requires some level of state-certified training. I've found that nine times out of ten, a licensed salesperson puts more effort into his or her ongoing education about timeshare real estate than does a nonlicensed salesperson. Know that you're entitled to ask whether a license is needed in that particular state or country and are equally entitled to ask whether your salesperson is fully accredited and licensed. If a license is required and your salesperson doesn't have one, you're within your rights to politely ask for a salesperson who is licensed. Shame on resorts who maintain nonlicensed salespersons in states where a license is required.

### Will the salesperson be "showing" more than one price?

I don't know how you feel about this, but I want to be told the actual price of whatever product I am considering buying. In other words, I don't like it when the salesperson shows me an initial figure of $40,000, and every time I say "it's too expensive," $2,500 is lopped off the price or the manager miraculously finds something I may be interested in for significantly less money. At worst, it's a sham; at best it's a way of testing you to see whether you're interested.

Now, you may enjoy the art of the deal: negotiating the price and playing the haggling game. Fine. If you don't, you're entitled to ask ahead of time whether the salesperson will be showing more than one price or whether the price stays the same.

You're in control of what happens at this sales presentation. Until and unless you pull out your wallet, nothing happens.

### Is the property I am being shown the same one I am asked to purchase?

Although many timeshares are still sold as *dirt* or *pre-construction,* my advice is to purchase only a product you have actually been shown.

Timeshare developed its rather seedy reputation some 30 years ago, when the timeshare market in the United States was young and something of a rarity. Thousands of people bought what turned out to be swampland after being shown an artist's rendering of the future timeshare. In many cases, nothing was built, and developers absconded with millions of dollars.

These days, with the hotel brands and big-name resorts bringing to the timeshare market their solid reputations and reputable business practices, the old swampland scam is fading from view. Nevertheless, when it comes to spending thousands of dollars on a vacation product that is still in the dirt stage, "buyer beware" is a good rule to follow.

## *What are the fees — all of the fees?*

Fees and rules vary from resort to resort. Some of the general extras include down payment, interest rate, term of loan, monthly payment, maintenance fees, real estate taxes, special assessments, membership fees, upgrade fees, and automatic debit fees. Always ask to see everything — the prices, maintenance fees, membership fees, interest rates, prepayment penalties — *in writing* before signing anything.

After you have everything in writing, ask which fees are negotiable. I'm not saying you should turn the deal down if the resort refuses to waive the exchange company's membership fee; I'm saying that it doesn't hurt to ask. Also remember that many of these fees are annual. A $99 membership fee to the exchange company may not seem like a large amount of money, but after 20 years, you're looking at shelling out more than $2,000 (plus, they increase periodically).

## *When should I make reservations to use my timeshare?*

Timeshare works on supply and demand and timing. Common sense rules. If you were planning to get a hotel room in New Orleans for Mardi Gras week, how long in advance would you make your reservations? One year? One month? One week? Walk in? I hope you said "one year." The

---

# Of sundries and snack bars

"We own multiple weeks at the same resort and return there year after year. Here are some of the things we like about our timeshare, and things you may want to ask about before buying:

✔ How close are the nearest restaurants, grocery stores, and hospitals?

✔ Does the resort have a restaurant/snack bar/bar and/or sundries shop on the property?

✔ Are safes available in the rooms?

✔ Are there shuttles to any area attractions and are they free?

✔ What activities are on the property and are there fees?

Our resort has activities for children as well as adults, which we never took the time to ask about, and our salesperson never pointed out, but which we really like.

We also recommend getting to know the property manager at the resort. Because we return year after year, it's like coming to our second home. Everyone knows us."

Jerry and Elaine Kleever, Curtis, Ohio

same holds true for timeshare. If, on the other hand, you were looking for a hotel in a less-popular destination in a low-demand season, how long in advance would you make your reservations? The answer is you probably don't have to rush, because the demand is simply not there.

The rule in timeshare is this: Always make your reservations as far in advance as possible to ensure that you have the widest choice of resorts. Both of the major exchange companies advise you to provide two or three choices of resorts and two or three choices of arrival date to maximize your chances of getting what you want. If you own in a low-demand area, you need to make your reservations longer in advance than if you own in a high-demand area. Even owning a timeshare in a high-demand destination like Orlando or Las Vegas doesn't mean you're guaranteed anything. If you know where you want to be six months ahead of time, book it! Remember also that in a fixed week system, you generally don't need to make reservations at your home resort — but check in advance to make sure.

## Second-Tier Questions

Although I refer to these as the non-deal-breaker questions, the following issues can be just as important to buyers as the bigger concerns.

### Will I own a specific unit or "a" unit?

At some resorts this is a very important distinction; at others, it's not. If, for example, you purchase at a beachfront resort in California, you may request an oceanview unit, particularly if that's the model you were shown. Make sure, if you're purchasing a timeshare unit you haven't been shown, that you get what you want. You don't want to assume you purchased oceanview and find out that your condo is identical to the one you were shown, albeit with a view overlooking the parking lot.

### What is included in the condo?

How many televisions does the unit have? What type of furniture is there and how many beds does it have? What are the available kitchen appliances and tableware? How many sets of towels and sets of bed linens are available? What, if any, are the fees for additional towels or additional bed linens?

Use the checklist in Table 7-1 to see exactly what you're getting.

| Table 7-1 | Timeshare Amenity Checklist | |
|---|:---:|---|
| *Amenity* | ✔ | *Comments* |
| Beds | ❏ | |
| King | ❏ | |
| Queen | ❏ | |
| Double | ❏ | |
| Single | ❏ | |
| Television(s) | ❏ | |
| Basic | ❏ | |
| Cable | ❏ | |
| VCR(s) | ❏ | |
| DVD(s) | ❏ | |
| Stereo(s) | ❏ | |
| Computer(s) | ❏ | |
| Internet access | ❏ | |
| Charges | ❏ | |
| Telephone(s) | ❏ | |
| Charges | ❏ | |
| Fax machines | ❏ | |
| Charges | ❏ | |
| Full-size refrigerator | ❏ | |
| Small-size refrigerator | ❏ | |
| Toaster | ❏ | |
| Blender | ❏ | |
| Breadmaker | ❏ | |
| Can opener | ❏ | |
| Electric | ❏ | |
| Manual | ❏ | |
| Stove/oven | ❏ | |
| Gas | ❏ | |
| Electric | ❏ | |
| Microwave | ❏ | |
| Tableware | ❏ | |
| Washing machine/dryer | ❏ | |
| In room | ❏ | |
| On floor | ❏ | |
| On property | ❏ | |
| Hair dryer | ❏ | |
| Towels | ❏ | |
| Linens | ❏ | |
| Miscellaneous | ❏ | |

## Does the resort supply a starter package of kitchen supplies?

Many resorts supply a "starter package" of supplies, which usually includes dish soap, dishwashing detergent, laundry detergent, trash bags, sugar/sweetener, paper towels, coffee filters, tea bags, coffee, salt and pepper, and the like.

## Do I have to use the same towels in the room and at the pool(s) or beach(es)?

If not, is there a fee for towel usage? Is there a limit on how many towels are allocated per guest?

## What is the housekeeping policy?

Find out how often the rooms are cleaned during your stay and what a cleaning consists of. Are the linens changed every day? Is there a housekeeping fee? Can you decline housekeeping if you don't want it? How are housekeeping fees and gratuities paid? Can you use your points if you want to?

## Does the resort offer rental services for extra days?

Many resorts have specific days of the week that are referred to as *check-in days*. For many, check-in days are Friday, Saturday, and/or Sunday. If you want to pay for an extra night, does the resort allow you to rent a room? What are the fees for renting this room? How long in advance do you need to make rental reservations as opposed to your regular week?

## Will the resort offer to rent my week out if I decide not to use it that year?

Many resorts offer this as a service to their owners. Be sure to find out how much the resort rents for, and what fees, if any, the resort charges to act as your agent. Also find out how long in advance you should let the resort know that you want the unit rented. If they do rent it for you, will you be paid cash or is the money applied to your account? How soon after the rental will you receive your payment?

## What are the meal or dining options at the resort?

Do they offer room service? If so, what is the fee? Does the resort have restaurants on the property? Do you receive a discount at these restaurants? Are the restaurants open to the public (see the following section for more on this)? Do you receive discounts at any nearby restaurants?

### Are the resort's facilities open to nonowners?

Do nonowners (area locals) have access to resort amenities such as the restaurants, the spa, or the golf course? (To some, this is not a good thing, unless the nonowners are being charged to use the facilities, fees that could possibly go toward maintenance.) In the same vein, are all the resort amenities available to the owners or are extra fees involved?

### Are phone, fax, and Internet services available? What are the fees for using them?

Many resorts are now offering Internet-ready rooms. Be sure to ask about the phone charges associated with this service and any other phone or fax charges.

### What are the hours of the front desk?

Surprisingly, many front desks at timeshares aren't open 24 hours a day. If the front desk is closed part of the day, ask for the telephone number of the off-site contact person in the event that you need help.

### What are the hours of the maintenance department?

Clogged sinks and leaky toilets rarely happen at opportune moments. Timeshares should have 24-hour maintenance coverage; be sure to ask whether yours does.

### What sort of transportation is available?

Are there shuttles or taxis to area attractions? What is the cost? How often do these run per day? Is pick-up and delivery to the airport available? How much does this cost? When do reservations have to be made?

## Talk to the locals

"Before I consider buying a timeshare, I like to get a feel for a place, what it's like to live there. I do that by talking to the locals. The check-in people at the resort are usually nice and often helpful. But the local people at the area grocery stores, shops in town, and gas stations often give you better information about local sights and activities. Want to know what is special about the area you are visiting? Like to go to yard sales? Into antiques? Want to know the cheapest place to buy gas? Like to hike, bowl, roller-blade, do needlepoint? Want the visit the best Mexican restaurant? Ask the locals. Also, check the local newspapers. But talking to the locals is often the best bet."

George Humfeld, Reston, Virginia

## *How close are the nearest stores, restaurants, banks and/or ATMs?*

Are shops within walking distance or are there shuttles, buses, or taxis available for transportation? If the resort has an ATM, is there a fee for using your bank's card?

## *What extra services does the resort offer?*

Larger timeshare resorts often have a full-service concierge on the property to assist you with car rentals, attraction ticket purchases, sightseeing tours, and the like. Note that the resort listings in both II and RCI directories (see Chapter 12) come with a full *legend,* detailing which services and amenities that resort contains.

# Chapter 8

# Financing Your Timeshare

● ● ● ● ● ● ● ● ● ● ● ● ● ● ● ● ● ● ● ● ● ● ● ● ● ● ● ● ● ● ● ● ● ● ● ● ● ● ● ● ● ● ● ● ●

## *In This Chapter*

▶ Finding ways to finance your timeshare

▶ Discovering alternative payment methods

● ● ● ● ● ● ● ● ● ● ● ● ● ● ● ● ● ● ● ● ● ● ● ● ● ● ● ● ● ● ● ● ● ● ● ● ● ● ● ● ● ● ● ● ●

*Y*ou may be very close to buying timeshare offered by a resort development company. Perhaps you've attended the sales presentation, asked the hard questions (see Chapter 7), and gotten the right answers. The location is just right, the condo is the perfect size, the amenities are right up your alley. You're ready to purchase. Now you have to determine how you plan to pay for it all.

 Make sure the price is the lowest the timeshare salesperson will go. Some timeshares and salespeople *show* (offer) inflated figures to start in order to test your willingness to purchase. I've seen salespeople show a $17,900 price on a one-bedroom timeshare that I was showing at $9,900. (Personally, I don't believe in playing price games with the prices; I don't believe in wasting my time or undermining a buyer's intelligence.)

Should you ask for a lower price? Yes! You have nothing to lose and good money to gain.

 Never underestimate the ability of salespeople to be sloppy with math. Ask to borrow a calculator (or bring your own) and double-check all the figures. If you find an error or a fee you just don't understand, politely point out the error or discreetly ask to speak with a manager. Anyone who is asking you to spend several thousands of dollars should be able to show you the correct figures.

For more on understanding the basic economics of timeshare, go to Chapter 3. For information on buying resale property, see Chapter 9.

---

## Who sells timeshare?

From "Resort Timesharing in U.S.," prepared by market researcher Ragatz Associates, comes the following data about the source of timeshare:

- ✔ From a developer: 73%

- ✔ Resale from a current owner: 15%

- ✔ From a property owner association: 8%

- ✔ Inherited, received as a gift, and other: 4%

---

## *Coming Up with a Financing Plan*

There are several ways to go about financing your timeshare purchase. At some point you have to come up with a down payment (see the following section). But before getting to that, you need to know that if you decide to make monthly payments to the timeshare company, you'll be charged 15.9% interest, while average mortgage rates are about 6%. Why is the interest rate so high? The interest rate is calculated at 15.9% basically because anyone who walks into a timeshare qualifies for financing. Unfortunately, the consumer is the one who pays the price for this everyone-qualifies deal.

Take a look at the average price of timeshare to give you some financing options:

| | |
|---|---|
| Purchase price: | $13,500 |
| 10% down payment: | $1,350 |
| Closing costs: | $500 |
| Total due today: | $1,850 |
| Amount financed: | $12,150 |
| (15.9% for 84 months) | |
| Monthly payment: | $240.63 |
| Total amount paid in 84 months: | $20,212.92 |

You can pay the monthly payments for 84 months and make the timeshare resort very happy, because it stands to make a lot of money. But you have other options:

> ✔ **Take out a home equity loan or home equity line of credit.** While some resorts will work with you to lower the 15.9% interest rate, in most cases, your best bet is to refinance the purchase (less the

down payment) when you get home. Whatever amount of money you can get from a home equity loan or line of credit will be less than what the timeshare is charging you for interest.

Most timeshares offer what is called *simple interest with no penalty for prepayment.* If you plan to refinance this way, ask the salesperson to delay the first monthly payment as long as possible (30 to 45 days is normal) and make sure the paperwork clearly states that there is no penalty for paying the timeshare off early. An added bonus of refinancing this way is that in most cases, the interest you pay on the home equity loan or line of credit is tax deductible.

This book is not meant to represent the letter of the law in every single jurisdiction. If you live in Texas, for example, you probably already know that home equity loans and home equity lines of credit can be used only for your primary residence, so a loan like this used to finance a timeshare is *not* tax deductible.

✔ **Pay more than the required amount each month.** If you can't refinance the loan and still don't want to pay the high interest rate, ask the salesperson to verify that the loan doesn't carry a penalty for early payment. For example, if you pay just $25 extra each month on the example previously shown (for a total of $265.63), and apply the extra money to the principal amount, you reduce the term of the loan from seven years (84 months) to about four years and eight months (56 months) and reduce the effective interest from 15.9% to about 8.3%.

# The first-hour-of-the-day payment method

No other options? Suppose you have no way of paying for the timeshare at this time other than accepting the high interest rate. How are you going to come up with the monthly payment without decreasing the quality of your life? You can try the *first-hour-of-the-day* method.

For this example, I assume you make $17 per hour, which works out to $35,360 per year. Take the first hour of each day you work ($17) and set aside that money to pay for your timeshare.

$17 per day × 5 days a week × 4 weeks

$85 per week × 4 weeks = $340 per month

At this rate, you may be able to pay off your timeshare in less than seven years and at a lower interest rate than you originally thought. Again, be sure to get in writing that there is no penalty for early payment.

✓ **Pay in cash or by credit card.** Most timeshares give you a slight discount on the price for paying in cash. Although in most cases you lose any tax deduction, there are cases where you benefit. For example, if you pay for the timeshare with a credit card that gives you double airline miles or other such perks, and your interest rate on the credit card is less than what the timeshare is charging you, go for it.

## The Down Payment

Many timeshare salespersons show (offer) an initial down payment of 20%. In most cases, however, the standard industry down payment is 10% — and in some cases even lower. So always be sure to ask whether the down payment is negotiable. In most instances, it is.

## Getting an Instant Credit Card

At more and more resorts, the big exchange companies are offering an "instant" credit card to use for everyday purchases to amass rewards that are redeemable for travel, hotels, rental cars, merchandise, and cash. You may even be able to use one, after you're approved, for an on-the-spot down payment on your timeshare.

✓ **RCI Elite Awards credit card:** With the Elite Awards credit card, you earn one reward for every $1 you spend on purchases. You also earn bonus rewards when you use the credit card for purchases at RCI and selected partners. You can redeem your rewards for travel, entertainment, retail, dining, and other items. Keep in mind that RCI Elite Awards and RCI Points are two separate programs. Rewards earned through the RCI Elite Awards program cannot be transferred directly to your RCI Points account, and points in your RCI Points account cannot be transferred or used within your RCI Elite Rewards account.

✓ **II WorldPoints Visa credit card:** II has also instituted a credit card that awards one point for every $1 in retail purchases. You can apply for the credit card at the timeshare sales center: You fill out a credit application, and if approved, the down payment is put directly on the card. You can redeem your points for travel, hotels, rental cars, cruises, merchandise, and cash.

This is all very convenient, but keep in mind that instant credit or not, you still have to pay off the credit card (including interest rates!) and bear responsibility for the full cost of the timeshare.

# Chapter 9

# Buying Resale and through Referral Programs

*R*esale is everywhere these days. Just type the word **timeshare** into your computer browser's search engine, and you come up with numerous Web sites advertising timeshare resales. One afternoon, in fact, I got 5,534 results advertising resale timeshare. Wow: That's almost more than the total number of timeshares in existence.

Timeshare is a commercial product and, as such, should be sold to consumers like any other product, through not just one outlet (you know, sales presentations) but through as many outlets as the market will bear. I believe that you, the consumer, should be able to buy this product new or used, in person or online, and from developers as well as from owners.

If you're going to buy resale, first do your research. Find out exactly what you're getting before you take the plunge. This chapter helps you understand the ins and outs of buying resale, find resale values, and discover the benefit of referrals.

## Buying Secondary Market Timeshares

Consider a "used" or resale timeshare in much the same way as you consider a used car. The car is either on the market because it didn't work the way the original owner needed it to, or the original owner found a newer car on the market with more options. Should you buy the car? If the car doesn't shift into drive, then no matter what the price, you shouldn't buy it. If the car doesn't come with power steering and you want power steering, again, you shouldn't buy it.

A good percent of timeshare is out on the resale market for what I consider to be legitimate reasons:

- ✔ Someone has died
- ✔ Someone is getting divorced
- ✔ Someone can't make the payments
- ✔ Someone isn't using it enough
- ✔ Someone's needs have changed

These legitimate reasons allow you to find good deals in the timeshare resale market, but first, you have to be willing to invest some time and effort researching options and comparing costs.

Of course, if the price is very, very low, you may just want to take the plunge: If you stumble across a week of timeshare just about anywhere short of a fractious, war-torn country for, say, $1,500 — assuming the maintenance and taxes are up to date and the resort meets your standards — you would have to use that timeshare only two or three times for it to pay for itself, and you could then turn around and sell it again.

So, should you buy resale? It depends on what you want to do with it. Some of what is out there on the resale market is for sale because it doesn't work, or it doesn't work as well as other timeshares now available.

## Factoring in exchange power

If Bob and Vera bought a week of off-season timeshare in a lovely lakeside retreat in Missouri and believed that they would be able to trade the week anytime they wanted for a week in Hawaii, Aruba, Orlando, or Paris, they will be understandably upset, because their timeshare does not have the trading power of the more popular resorts. They may have paid $8,000 for this week of timeshare, but after four years of being told "no" by the exchange company, Bob and Vera may decide they've had enough: They want to sell their two-bedroom timeshare in Missouri. They put it on the market for only $4,000.

One day, as you're thumbing through timeshare resale advertisements, one ad jumps out at you: "Stunning two-bedroom timeshare located in the heart of the Lake of the Ozarks. Sleeps six, full kitchen, six pools at resort. Paid $8,000 originally, will sacrifice for only $4,000. Call today."

"Wow," you think. "Originally $8,000, now only $4,000." You call the resort in question, and (if they give you prices over the phone, which most resorts will not do) they tell you that two-bedroom timeshares are now going for $10,000. Sounds like your $4,000 timeshare is a steal.

It can be: It all depends on what you want to do with the timeshare. Do you want to trade to be able to exchange your timeshare week to visit high-demand destinations like Hawaii, Aruba, Orlando, and/or Paris? It may be very difficult to do so — and even though you paid half of what Bob and Vera paid, buying a Missouri timeshare may not be worth the money.

On the other hand, if you want nothing more than to visit the Lake of the Ozarks in the off-season for the next ten years or so, this week of timeshare becomes a bargain. Each week of vacation in a two-bedroom condo will cost you only $400, plus maintenance fees.

## Uncovering bargains that may not be bargains

Here's another scenario: Suppose Bob and Vera haven't used their time-share in four years and also haven't paid their maintenance and taxes in that time. Now, that $4,000 bargain that you think you are getting may end up costing you $6,000, $7,000, or more. This would be an example of when to say "no" to buying resale. Always ask the owners and timeshare management whether the maintenance fees are up to date.

Here's another example of a bargain that's not really a bargain. Shawn and Amy bought a two-bedroom in-season week in Orlando five years ago for $10,000. That resort is now selling those exact same timeshare condos for $18,000. Shawn and Amy are selling their timeshare for only $9,000. Should you buy it?

On the surface, it looks good. The timeshare is located in a high-demand area, a two-bedroom condo is just what you need to accommodate your family, and you would obviously rather pay $9,000 than $18,000. But here's the rub: Shawn and Amy have a "fixed" week, and that week is the third week of September.

✔ First of all, do you want to vacation every year on the third week in September? Can your kids take time off school then? Can you always get that week off work?

✔ Second, with a fixed-week program, you have the advantage of returning to your home resort each year with no reservations needed for that week. But if you're interested in trading, the resort only has the capabilities of putting that particular week into the reservation pool. The third week of September in Orlando is not as high in demand as, say, the first week of July. So, your trading or exchange power may go down considerably, and you may find out, as Shawn and Amy did, that you don't want a fixed week at all; you need a floating week. For more on fixed and floating weeks, see Chapter 7.

In almost all cases, when you purchase a points-based timeshare, or a timeshare affiliated with a brand name (see Chapter 13) from someone other than the developer, you can't take advantage of the points and any perks that come with the primary purchase. What you will own will be a standard week(s). Always ask.

## Advantages of buying resale

"We've owned a timeshare since the early '80s. Personally, now that we've had some experience in the field, I'd certainly recommend that anyone contemplating a timeshare purchase do so on the secondhand or resale market. Almost any resort and facility you can name has units for sale for a great deal less than the prices offered by the resort and/or its agents. Some resorts even have a resale office on the premises. Another good source for resales and information on timesharing in general is *TimeSharing Today* magazine (www.tsdoday.com) and the Tri-West Timeshare Auctions (www.triwest-timeshare.com), usually held every six months or so.

"And most important: Don't buy a unit at any resort until you've stayed there and experienced firsthand what the facilities and amenities are."

Gordon P. Cress, Carlsbad, California

### *Asking the right questions*

Buying used timeshare requires just as much due diligence as buying a timeshare from the developer. In addition to asking all the right questions (see Chapter 7), make sure you also get the answers to the following when buying resale:

- ✔ Are the maintenance and taxes up to date?

- ✔ Why is the timeshare being sold?

- ✔ Has the timeshare already been used this current year?

- ✔ Can the exchange company membership name be transferred or changed?

- ✔ Do all the benefits transfer (travel discounts, bonus or getaway weeks, and the like)?

- ✔ If the timeshare in question is points-based, does the ability to use these points transfer?

- ✔ Am I buying this timeshare from the owner, a resale company, the developer/resort, or a third party?

- ✔ What buying fees will I have to pay?

- ✔ If it's deeded property, who will be paying the closing costs?

- ✔ If it's deeded property, has a title search been done? Can a title search be done? Who pays for the title search?

- ✔ If it is a right-to-use property, how many more uses are left in it? Are the uses yearly as in one week for 20 years, for example, or are the uses total, as in 20 weeks of usage before it expires?

✔ Can I see the actual property and the actual condo in question?

✔ Is the condo in question in a newer or older section of the resort? Are all the amenities at the resort available to all the sections?

# Where to Find Resale Timeshare

These days, where there are classifieds, there is resale timeshare. I advise turning to those consumer sources that have built a loyal following among timeshare owners.

## Timeshare publications

If you're looking for resale timeshare, here are a few sources that I recommend:

✔ *TimeSharing Today* **magazine** (www.tsdoday.com): In addition to well-written articles, thorough resort reviews, and a wealth of information about current issues in the timeshare world, *Timesharing Today* has a good classifieds section listing timeshare resales and rentals, both domestic and international.

✔ **Timeshare Resale Alliance** (www.resaletimeshare.com): What I like about this group is that it deals only with those California timeshare resorts they have personal knowledge of. They operate much like a consulting service in that they take the time to find out what works for you, and then recommend one or more specific resales available.

✔ **Timeshare Tips** (www.tstips.com): In addition to finding timeshares for sale, Timeshare Tips has representatives from four exchange companies online answering questions for their members. In their words, "We recognize that all participants are necessary for a healthy timeshare industry. Although most of our members buy resale, we all recognize that without developer sales, there would be no resales. We also believe that without the ability to resell, developer sales would be more difficult."

✔ **Timeshare Users Group** (www.tug2.net): This online self-help group of timeshare owners (a fiercely loyal group who call themselves *Tuggers*) was formed in 1993 to provide, as the group says, "an unbiased source of consumer-oriented information regarding timeshare." It has a large classifieds section offering a growing list of resale timeshares as well as timeshare for rent, sale, and exchange. To join, a membership fee of $15 is required for the first 12 months, and it's $10 a year to renew.

✔ *The Timeshare Beat* (www.thetimesharebeat.com): The Beat is the timeshare industry's most-read online publication. It has many articles about timeshare and is free. The Beat has a nice section on frauds.

## eBay and other online auctions

Okay, I admit it; I'm an eBay novice. I've never bought or sold anything on the wildly successful online auction marketplace — until now, when I logged on to eBay (www.ebay.com) and typed in the word **timeshare**. I was astounded by what I found.

It turns out that eBay has tons of timeshare listings. Some sound too good to be true. Some sound so good that I'm tempted to bid. For example, here is an actual (although now closed) listing, with the brand name and seller information not listed:

**LAS VEGAS (Name of Resort) Floating RED Timeshare**

Current bid: $299.00

History: 1 bid (US $299.00 starting bid)

High bidder: Not available

Item location: Las Vegas, NV, United States

The copy read as follows:

LOOK NO FURTHER, INVEST ONCE AND VACATION FOR A LIFETIME. Here is your chance to own a DEEDED (Does Not Expire) Property at a bargain price. This RCI, HOSPITALITY RATED, One Bedroom, One Bath, that sleeps Four (Terrace Bldg) is an ANNUAL FLOATING RED Week 6-17. The (resort name) is located in Las Vegas, NV and is an RCI RESORT. The annual maintenance fees and taxes are $395. All fees are current with the mortgage paid in full. Your annual usages and fees starts this year's and the new owner will be responsible for 2005 maintenance fees at Closing. Prime Location gives you maximum trading power with RCI, giving you the ability to choose from over 3500 resorts worldwide, should you decide to exchange your week. Check In Day is Sunday, NO RESERVE!!

It followed a description of the timeshare unit, amenities offered, check-in procedures, the color code, the week, the number of bedrooms, square footage, maintenance fees, and address. The listing ended with:

Questions gladly answered. About Closing: Closing and escrow to be handled with (name of company), a licensed, insured, and bonded Escrow/Title Company of Orlando, FL. A $500 deposit is due after auction ends, with balance due at closing. There is a transfer fee of $75. Closing costs are $330, which include Escrow, Deed preparation, recording fees, and resort notification of transfer of ownership. Personal Checks, Money Order, or Cashier's Check Only to open escrow. TOTAL MONIES DUE: Bid Price + Transfer Fee $75 + Closing Cost $330 + Maintenance Fees + $395 = TOTAL COST.

So I thought, if I had bid $300 and won, I would have picked up a Red-coded floating week in Las Vegas for only $1,100 — or about $8,500 less than I would normally expect to pay. Each year I would be paying $395 for maintenance and taxes plus $139 to exchange my week somewhere else. Was there any reason *not* to buy it? So I e-mailed the seller these questions and received these answers:

**Q.** Why are you selling this timeshare?

**A.** I buy and resell timeshare.

**Q.** How long have you owned it?

**A.** I have owned this for about 3 months.

**Q.** The current bid is $299.00 . . . is this your minimum bid?

**A.** I have no reserve on this property, so the highest bidder wins the auction.

**Q.** Is this RCI points, and if so, how many points would I receive yearly?

**A.** This is not RCI points; it would have to be converted into RCI points.

Now my interest was really piqued. So I printed out the eBay listing and asked some friends of mine who sell new timeshare (that is, from a developer) if this was indeed a legitimate offering.

Everyone responded the same way: Provided that the maintenance and taxes are up to date, there is no good reason not to purchase this time-share. Several people even asked for the information to bid on the unit themselves!

The closing and escrow on this timeshare was being handled out of a company in Orlando, Florida. I called the company and spoke with some-one who answered all of my questions and even e-mailed me an extensive eight-page document that went into great detail about the company's services. I was doing this only for research, so I didn't put in an offer, but I believe this would have been a good purchase.

So, why not search eBay or other online auction clearinghouse service for timeshare when you sometimes can get them for thousands less than buying from the developer? The answer is simple: Provided you know the right questions to ask and understand the concept of timeshare, there's no reason not to use these Internet sources. Buying timeshare online demands that you do the same basic homework you would do when buying from a developer.

# Buying through Referral Programs

Many resorts offer owners the benefits of a referral program. A *referral program* is what it sounds like: Owners earn certain benefits for referring their friends, family, and co-workers to their timeshare resort.

## Referrals: A win-win situation

I have only praise for referral programs. Everyone — the original owner, the resort, the salesperson, and the referral — wins. Here's how:

- ✔ **The timeshare owner:** If you're the owner, you earn something for merely providing the resort with names, phone numbers, addresses, and/or e-mail addresses of other people who like to travel.

- ✔ **The resort:** The resort wins because it doesn't have to spend any money to market to these referrals. The resort doesn't do the marketing anyway; it hires marketing companies to do that, and in my opinion the marketing companies don't understand target marketing. (For more on how timeshares are marketed, see Chapter 5.)

- ✔ **The salesperson:** The salesperson wins because he or she has a client who has heard only good things about the resort and doesn't need to be sold with long sales presentations.

- ✔ **The referral:** If you're the referral — that is, you have friends or family who have referred you to a particular resort — you win because, unlike many people who end up at the timeshare marketing presentation after being sold a discounted vacation package or being bribed with free attraction tickets or dinner, you're at the resort to take advantage of something that friends, family, or co-workers recommend and enjoy.

As a salesperson, my clients like me enough and trust me enough to know that just as I don't high-pressure them, I will not high-pressure their referrals. I've even had clients invite me into their homes to present timeshare in a Tupperware party atmosphere. The referrals are relaxed. Come prepared with specific questions about the product, talk to the original owners, and leave feeling good about the entire process, regardless of whether they bought timeshare or not.

Bad news travels further and faster than good news, so if you're pleased with your timeshare, have had good experiences, like and trust your salesperson, and want to share your good experiences, use your referral program to the maximum. If for some reason, your timeshare resort doesn't have a referral program, insist that it initiates one.

## The benefits of referral programs

What sorts of benefits do resorts offer owners who provide referrals? Here are some examples:

✔ Discounts off the price shown. For example, a salesperson may say "The price of the two-bedroom unit is $15,000, but if you give us five referrals, we'll knock $1,000 off of that."

✔ Money for each referral who actually visits the resort — and more if that person purchases.

✔ Free or discounted exchange company memberships.

✔ Vouchers in lieu of actual money, which are sent to you or put in your account to be used for anything you can purchase at the resort — anything from drinks at the pool bar to paying your maintenance fees.

The benefits for referral programs can be creative according to the destination. For the Manhattan Club in New York, for example, some of the referral perks offered at press time include tickets to a Broadway show, dinner aboard a World Yacht cruise, and seven days accommodations plus round-trip airfare to any RCI or II resort in the continental United States.

# Chapter 10

# Buying International Timeshare

· · · · · · · · · · · · · · · · · · · · · · · · · · · · · · · · · · · · · · · · · ·

## In This Chapter

▶ Discovering the ins and outs of buying international timeshare

▶ Asking the right questions

▶ Buying international: A tale of two couples

· · · · · · · · · · · · · · · · · · · · · · · · · · · · · · · · · · · · · · · · · ·

*T*imeshare started overseas and today remains an international phenomenon: Of the more than 5,400 timeshare resorts worldwide, only 30% are located in the United States. International timeshare ranges from Australia to Zimbabwe, Austria to Mexico, and almost every country in-between.

Should you buy a timeshare outside the United States? With all the amazing choices, why not? You can easily trot the globe through timesharing, or, if you prefer, stay close to home at one of the many international choices nearby — including the Caribbean, Mexico, Central America, and Canada. If you're an urbanite who loves to visit the world's great cities, check out the growing urban interval ownership options (see Chapter 16). If you have the travel time to go great distances and you're the kind of vacationer who's interested in seeing a different part of the world each year, a timeshare exchange may be the way to go. For more on exchanging, see Chapter 12.

 Unlike timeshares in North America, the timeshare product in many parts of the world is a nondeeded right-to-use interest good only for a specified number of years. In other words, you won't actually share ownership of the resort's real estate. On the plus side, a right-to-use project may be less expensive than a deeded timeshare at a comparable resort somewhere else. Make sure to ask whether the property is deeded or nondeeded before you buy — and make sure you know how long it's yours to use.

Some people like to play the "buying to trade" game. They look for less expensive destinations to buy — even places they have no intention of ever visiting — largely for the trade value. At press time, companies in South Africa, for example, was selling timeshares on the beach, in

resorts, or in cities, at fairly reasonable prices. This can be fraught with risk, because the trading power of a lesser-priced resort may not be strong enough to get you the most desirable exchanges (exchange companies like to match like-to-like). For more on buying to trade, see Chapter 12.

Beware of impulse buying. As with timeshare in the United States, don't get caught up in the moment or seduced by the beauty of the resort. And keep your wits about you if you've signed on to a timeshare presentation. Weigh the pros and cons carefully before you sign *anything* on the dotted line.

## Buying to Stay versus Buying to Trade

Before you buy internationally in a place you plan to spend time, ask yourself some basic questions:

- ✔ If the language is foreign to you, do you feel comfortable reading, understanding, and speaking the language?

- ✔ Are you attuned to local culture and customs?

- ✔ Does the destination harbor potentially dangerous conditions, whether crime, civil unrest, or an undercurrent of hostility toward foreigners?

If you plan to use the timeshare more as an exchange property, do you have a basic understanding of worldwide travel patterns and trading economics? For example, Venice, Italy, is a prime place to purchase for trading power; 23 million people visit every year, and the city has only a handful of timeshare resorts — so its trade value is considerable. On the other hand, a timeshare in a minor travel destination — or one in a saturated timeshare market — may be less desirable as an exchange property.

Both RCI and II value trading power (see Chapter 12 for more on these two companies). A timeshare in Paris, France, may have far more trading power than a timeshare in Gautier, Mississippi. Does that mean you should buy a timeshare in Paris, France? Well, on the one hand, it will give you an excellent exchange, particularly if you own the weeks around Bastille Day (July 14, which is almost always also smack in the middle of the Tour de France). And if you plan to visit Paris numerous times, buying a timeshare may save you money on hotel rooms and restaurants in the long run.

On the other hand, your personal preferences and comfort level may weigh more on your decision than getting prime exchange property. Places like the Gulf Coast of Mississippi may be your idea of a great vacation — and more affordable as well — and you're happy to trade for like properties.

If you're interested in globe-trotting, look at timeshare exchange from a global perspective. Know that Orlando, Florida, is a global destination (drawing people from all over the world), whereas Myrtle Beach, South Carolina, is more of a regional destination.

## Asking the Right Questions

If you're ready to start your search, don't be afraid to ask tough questions. The savvy editors at *TimeSharing Today,* an independent online timeshare magazine, recommend that potential buyers of international property ask the following important questions:

> ✔ **How stable is the government at all levels — national, regional, and local?** Be sure to go to the U.S. State Department's Travel Warnings Web site (http://travel.state.gov) before considering any destination. This site reports on places where health concerns or unrest may threaten American travelers. Also contact the U.S. embassy in the country in which you're purchasing.
>
> ✔ **To what extent does the government regulate the timeshare industry?** If the government has no formal registration procedures for timeshare projects, similar to those that exist in the United States, carefully evaluate the developer's financial capabilities and reputation.
>
> ✔ **Has the government passed consumer-protection laws?** If so, do these laws cover timesharing, and what are your rights as a timeshare buyer under those laws?
>
> ✔ **With or without government regulation, has the industry in that country undertaken its own program of self-regulation?** Ask whether you as a consumer have any governmental protection against substandard construction materials and methods.
>
> ✔ **Will you receive a contract, resort rules and regulations, and other key documents in your own language or another language you know very well?** If not, beware of misunderstandings due to language differences.
>
> ✔ **Is title insurance available?** The answer is almost certainly "no" in a foreign right-to-use setting, and probably "no" even in most foreign deeded settings. (While many United States timeshares include property insurance in the yearly maintenance fees, there are thousands of documented cases where entire resorts in the Caribbean were wiped out due to hurricanes, leaving owners with an unusable deed, along with some sand and shells.)
>
> ✔ **Does the resort have a U.S. office?** If so, does it accept payments there in U.S. currency? Does it have a domestic toll-free telephone line on which you can discuss reservations and other aspects of ownership with someone in English?

↙ **Even without a U.S. office, can you pay for the timeshare in your own currency?** If you must pay in a foreign currency, anticipate currency-exchange fees, which can increase your costs significantly. Remember, too, that fluctuations in currency values may work in your favor or against you. A foreign timeshare purchase can be a long-term commitment to pay maintenance fees, taxes, and whatever personal expenses you incur while in residence there. The positive or negative impact of dealing in a foreign currency will be with you for many years.

↙ **What taxes will you have to pay?** As a foreigner, are you being taxed differently from citizens of the country in which the timeshare is located?

↙ **What are your estimated maintenance fees?** In foreign locations where most foodstuffs and supplies for a resort must be imported at considerable cost, high operating expenses are likely and will be reflected in the maintenance fees.

↙ **Who will manage the resort?** The developer? An owners' association? A management firm? A local resident manager? Although management at the best foreign resorts meets or even exceeds the highest U.S. standards, horror stories also exist. Especially in a foreign land far from home, look for some assurance of competent management. Also, can you speak with someone at the resort at a convenient time for you when you need to? (Remember that other parts of the world may be many hours ahead or behind your local time zone.)

## Exchange rates and monthly payments

Anytime you're dealing with foreign currencies, you're taking risks with exchange rates. For Canadian and United Kingdom residents buying U.S. property, deciding whether to fix the monthly payments or not can make a big different in those payments.

For example, Marie and Claude live in Montreal, Quebec, and purchase a timeshare in Daytona Beach, Florida. Their monthly payments at the time of their purchase were US$100 per month, which translated to CA$135. However, their monthly payments are fixed at US$100, and because of the decreasing value of the Canadian dollar, monthly payments are now CA$185.

Shawn and Kim live in London, England, and purchase a timeshare in Las Vegas, Nevada. The monthly payments at the time of their purchase were US$100, which translated to £75. However, the monthly payments are not fixed at US$100, so despite the rising value of the British pound, their monthly payments stay the same. If they had asked for and received a fixed U.S. payment, their monthly fee would have dropped to £55 a month.

▶ **What is the exchange affiliation?** The best way to ensure decent trading power and a receptive ear if exchange-related problems arise is to look for a resort with a quality rating from either Interval International or RCI. See Chapter 12 for details.

## Buying Wrong: A Cautionary Tale

Toni and Allen live in Los Angeles, California. On a recent vacation to Cancun, they were invited to view a timeshare resort. The cordial salesperson met them, offered them a tequila drink, and proceeded to show them an immaculate resort — complete with three swimming pools, tennis courts, pool bars, and a luxurious one-bedroom condo with a terrace overlooking the water. Toni and Allen fell in love with the place as well as with Cancun. The salesperson took them back to the salesroom and showed them the price of the timeshare in Mexican pesos. Allen converted the price into American dollars and found that if they worked at it they could indeed pay for the timeshare. When they agreed to purchase the timeshare, the salesperson celebrated by offering another tequila. As they drank up, the salesperson brought out just three pieces of paperwork for Toni and Allen to sign. The paperwork was all in Spanish, which neither Toni nor Allen could read.

**Q:** Should Toni and Allen have bought this timeshare?

**A:** Of course not. As much as they like the resort and Cancun, one basic rule was broken immediately: Don't buy any timeshare if you're offered alcohol prior to or while signing anything.

More important, because Toni and Allen neither read nor understand Spanish, they had no way of knowing whether their timeshare is a deeded or a right-to-use or a fixed or floating week. They had no way to determine any specific legalities about the property or the resort.

## Buying Right: A Happy Tale

Cindi and Duane live in Cleveland, Ohio. They go on two vacations every year: one week each summer in Chicago to visit their grown daughter and one week each winter in the Austrian mountains to ski. On one visit to Austria, someone convinced them to look at a timeshare. It was a beautiful mountain retreat, with ski-in/ski-out facilities, ski instructors on staff, a full-service spa, and a restaurant serving the finest schnitzel they'd ever had. During the sales presentation, the salesperson spoke English and offered no alcohol. Cindi and Duane acknowledged that they really like the resort, felt comfortable there, understood the terms (the documents are all written in English), and felt they were willing to fit the expense into their budget. And even though this resort is a 20-year right-to-use property (meaning they will own it for only 20 years), they are tempted to sign up right then and there.

**Q:** Should Cindi and Duane have bought this timeshare?

**A:** Well, here's a summary:

- Cindi and Duane understood the terms.

- Cindi and Duane remained alcohol-free the entire time.

- Cindi and Duane planned on returning to this resort many more times in the future.

- Cindi and Duane felt confident that they could afford the timeshare.

Sounds like it was a great plan for Cindi and Duane to buy.

# Part III
# Discovering a World of Timeshare

The 5th Wave                    By Rich Tennant

"You and your big idea to buy a timeshare on one of the less-known Caribbean islands! Who ever heard of St. Bronx anyway?"

## *In this part . . .*

**T**imeshare is available around the globe, and this part tells
you exactly where you can expect to find it. I discuss the
nitty-gritty of exchanging timeshare so you can visit different
destinations around the world and what you can expect at the
brand-name resorts, which have entered the timeshare industry
in a big, impressive way.

# Chapter 11

# Location, Location, Location: Where the Timeshares Are

*W*ith more than 5,400 timeshare resorts located in 95 countries throughout the world, timeshare has a presence all over the globe — and good thing, too, for even the most remote corners of the world are getting easier and easier to reach. For people with limited vacation time and a limited budget, timeshare offers a practical way to see the world.

Timeshare comes in all shapes and forms, from condos to hotel suites to yachts to rooms in a chateau (for more examples of unique timeshare, go to Chapter 18). The same goes for locations. This chapter gives you a glimpse at the variety of timeshare destinations around the world, focusing on those places where the two major exchange companies, RCI and II, offer timeshare. The maps in this chapter also reflect only those destinations with RCI and II timeshare.

## Choosing the Right Location for You

First, determine whether the timeshare serves its purpose for you at a price you're willing to work into your budget.

# Snapshot: Orlando timeshare

Many consumers have their first taste of timeshare in and around Orlando. In their most recent catalogs, RCI listed 49 Orlando resorts, and II weighed in at 50. Some of the oldest timeshares in the United States, such as Orange Lake Country Club and Westgate Resorts, are located in the Orlando area. Marriott has six separate locations here, and of course, Disney Vacation Club is based here, with five separate resorts.

The often-misleading practice of *OPCing* (getting approached by off-property consultants who try to get you to sit through a presentation) is widespread in other areas, such as Las Vegas, Gatlinburg (Tennessee), Cancun, and the Bahamas, but in Orlando it has reached epidemic proportions. You simply cannot go into any retail or dining establishment on International Drive, Highway 535, or the most touristy stretch of road in the area, Highway 192, without being accosted. In Orlando, OPCs operate ticket/information booths scattered amid high-traffic tourist centers. They may try to entice you with discounted tickets or free dinners just for viewing a resort. Sometimes, the offers you receive from OPCs are legitimate — and sometimes they're scams. Often, the OPC is simply being paid by the person to bring bodies into timeshare resorts, regardless of a person's ability or interest in the product.

My mantra is: There is no such thing as a free lunch — or a free anything else, for that matter. At press time, the cost of a one-day admission to one of the major theme parks in Orlando is around $60. If you pull into a gas station on Highway 192 and see a poorly painted sign in front of a shabby booth that says, "TWO THEME PARK TICKETS $25 EACH!", warning bells should go off in your head. *All* of these places, every last one of 'em, are trying to pull you into a timeshare presentation. Many will say that the presentation lasts only 60 minutes, and virtually none of them will state that a timeshare presentation is required — instead describing the experience as a "vacation resort preview" or "a tour of our new vacation resort." Know what you are getting into before you sign on.

For me, Orlando exemplifies the very best and the very worst of timeshare. Here's why.

**The Good**

- **Location:** Although I've heard people complain that the plethora of timeshare weeks available makes Orlando a less-than-desirable trade, I find the opposite to be true. The reason big brands like Hilton, Marriott, Starwood, Westgate, and Disney (among others) continue to build timeshare units here is because of the ever-growing demand. Plus, owning in Orlando will generally get you what you want in trades.

- **Variety:** Almost every type of timeshare resort you can imagine exists or will soon exist in Orlando. Whether you want a resort with 90 holes of golf right on the property, a stunning three-bedroom home complete with private swimming pool, a wilderness retreat a short boat ride away from the Mouse himself, or an Italian villa steps away from a shopping mall, Orlando has it all.

## The Not-So-Good

✔ **People, people, and more people:** Unless you come to Orlando in January, early May, October, or the first two weeks of November, you'll find plenty of company at every resort. Orlando may not be the best place for a quiet, relaxing vacation, but it's definitely fun-filled.

✔ **"Resorts" that aren't close to being resorts:** No standard definition exists for the word *resort*—and the word is used loosely in Orlando. Some timeshare developers seem to think that if they plop a pool down beside a concrete condo, it's a resort, and I've seen many a renovated apartment complex optimistically referred to as a "resort." Be sure to ask all the important questions when buying or trading into a resort in Orlando.

✔ **Outdated marketing and sales practices:** In addition to the antiquated OPC system, Orlando is the scene of some of the most oft-repeated horror stories about timeshare salespersons. The cover of my first book, *Surviving A Timeshare Presentation . . . Confessions From The Sales Table,* featured the stereotypical image of a salesman with a big cigar in his mouth, wearing a tacky plaid jacket, and bearing a contract in hand — an image that in the olden days wasn't far from the truth. Unfortunately, the hard sell still exists in many of the most competitive markets, and it's a good idea to keep a clear head when evaluating timeshare in Orlando. Always refer to the first- and second-tier questions in Chapter 7.

Second, determine what you want your timeshare to do for you. Do you want to exchange or trade your timeshare with other timeshares in different locations? If so, you'll want to look for a timeshare in a location that will get you solid trading power. You may have to pay a little extra upfront to do so, but you may find that worthwhile down the road (although a few consumers have some degree of success playing the timeshare market like the stock market in what's called *buying to trade,* which means bagging desirable but inexpensive timeshare in little-known or up-and-coming destinations in the hopes that its exchange value gets more powerful over time; more about that in Chapter 12).

If, on the other hand, you plan to use your timeshare in the same location every year, ask yourself:

✔ What does the timeshare in the desired location have to offer? You may love a particular destination, but the resort you're looking at lacks the amenities you want and the type of timeshare you prefer.

✔ What features do you want your timeshare to have (how many bedrooms, for example, or maid service, or access to a golf course)?

✔ What are you willing to pay for it?

# Snapshot: New Orleans timeshare

If you like your vacations in places with lots of history and atmosphere, consider buying timeshare in The Big Easy: New Orleans, Louisiana. A visit to New Orleans is a trip back in time, where you dine alfresco in romantic antebellum courtyard restaurants, ride vintage trolley cars, and hear the clip-clop of horses' hooves on cobbled streets.

The major exchange companies, II and RCI, have staked out some prime Big Easy real estate. II has seven timeshare properties in New Orleans, and RCI has 13 — the majority of them are right in the middle of it the action, the French Quarter.

New Orleans properties are generally anything but the cookie-cutter high-rise condos found in many other places in the timeshare world. Although you won't find many two- or three-bedroom condos here, you can end up owning timeshare in an authentic 1830s townhouse built by pirates with well-appointed rooms and your own outdoor swimming pool with courtyard.

**Note:** If you plan to come to New Orleans during Mardi Gras or JazzFest, book a year in advance.

In the United States alone, there are 1,590 timeshare resorts, containing some 132,000 timeshare units. Table 11-1 gives you a breakdown of their locations.

### Table 11-1   Where Timeshare Is Located in the United States

| State | Number of Timeshares | Number of Units |
|---|---|---|
| Florida | 366 | 27,700 |
| California | 125 | 11,900 |
| South Carolina | 119 | 12,100 |
| Colorado | 75 | 6,250 |
| Hawaii | 73 | 4,830 |
| Virginia | (unknown) | 5,560 |
| North Carolina | 59 | 5,360 |
| Missouri | 49 | 5,530 |
| Nevada | 56 | 5,000 |
| Texas | 49 | (unknown) |
| Arizona | 46 | 4,640 |

*Florida Timeshare*

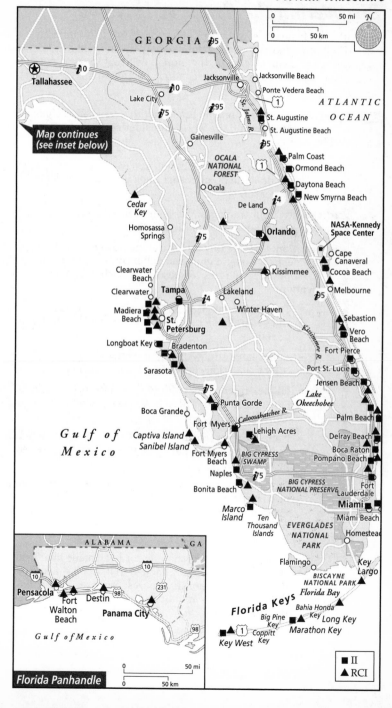

## Discovering the Power of Location

It's true in nearly every hospitality market in the vacation industry: The hotter, more appealing the location, the more in demand it will be — and, in all likelihood, the more it will cost to own. In most instances, the most popular locations command top prices on the timeshare market.

If you're interested in buying timeshare that you can exchange for other locations around the world, consider several variables before you buy:

- **Season:** Trading for the location and week you desire will be easier to do if the home resort week you own is in a high-demand season.

- **Quality:** Your trading power is maximized by the basic quality of your resort and the amenities it offers.

- **Location:** If you're buying for trading power, consider owning in a desirable destination that will prove easy to exchange. Here are some general rules to keep in mind when choosing your location:

  - Timeshares situated **on the water** (ocean, lake, marinas) will generally be more costly than timeshares situated inland.

  - Timeshares situated **on golf courses** will generally be higher priced than timeshares that have no golf course.

  - **Higher-rated resorts** (Gold Crown Resorts within RCI and Five-Star Resorts within II) will generally be priced higher than lower-rated resorts.

  - **Name-brand resorts** (such as Disney) will often be priced higher than non-brand-name resorts in the same geographic area.

  - Timeshare resorts located in **areas catering to affluent tourists** (Whistler, British Columbia, for example) will generally be priced higher than timeshare resorts located in areas catering to less affluent tourists (Cocoa Beach, Florida).

  - Just because a timeshare has a swell name like "VILLA", or "ROYALE", or "GRANDE" attached to it, don't think that makes it better than other timeshares. Names — other than reputable brands — are not an indication of quality in the timeshare world.

*California Timeshare*

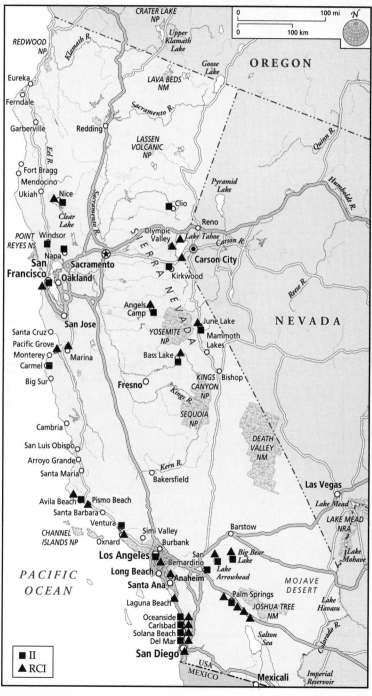

*Caribbean Timeshare*

FLORIDA

○ Miami

*Straits of Florida*

Havana
○

THE
BAHAMAS

CUBA

Little Cayman

Grand Cayman

Cayman Brac

CAYMAN ISLANDS

HAITI

Port-au-Prince ○

Montego Bay ○

JAMAICA    ○ Kingston

G R E A T E R

*Caribbean Sea*

■ II
▲ RCI

N

| 0 | 300 mi |

| 0 | 300 km |

COLOMBIA

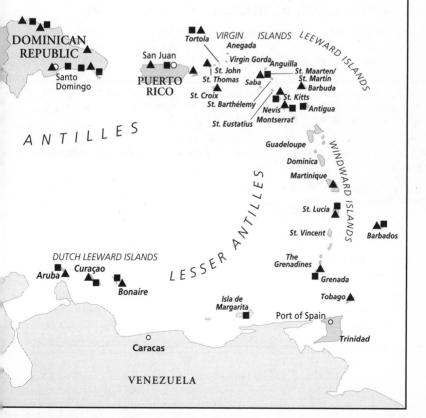

ATLANTIC
OCEAN

TURKS AND CAICOS ISLANDS

DOMINICAN
REPUBLIC

Santo
Domingo

San Juan

PUERTO
RICO

St. Croix

Tortola

VIRGIN ISLANDS LEEWARD ISLANDS
Anegada
Virgin Gorda Anguilla
St. John
St. Thomas Saba
St. Barthélemy
St. Eustatius

St. Maarten/
St. Martin
Barbuda
St. Kitts
Nevis Antigua
Montserrat

ANTILLES

Guadeloupe

Dominica

Martinique

WINDWARD ISLANDS

St. Lucia

LESSER ANTILLES

St. Vincent

Barbados

DUTCH LEEWARD ISLANDS

Aruba Curaçao

Bonaire

The
Grenadines

Grenada

Tobago

Isla de
Margarita

Port of Spain

Trinidad

Caracas

VENEZUELA

If you wish to exchange or trade your timeshare, keep in mind that the power of your exchange is based solely on what you put into the system, not what you take out. In other words, what you own is the most important factor in determining whether you will receive the exchange that you want.

The two major exchange companies, RCI and II, have resorts worldwide. To see the specific locations for each company, see Tables 11-2 and 11-3. Chapter 12 goes into much more detailed information about how these exchange companies evaluate and rank timeshare and determine the power of your exchange.

Although timeshares are ranked and rated on their trading power, don't discount the power of personal preferences. A high-season week in Orlando may be popular, but a vacation there may mean nothing to you. Many people may prefer the solitude of a hillside retreat at a low-demand, low-season week in Missouri, say. That's what makes the trading game always unpredictable and ever entertaining.

---

# Snapshot: Venice, Italy, timeshare

The Queen of the Adriatic has fascinated visitors for hundreds of years. Venice is comprised of a series of more than 1,700 islands of various sizes. The city is filled with more art, museums, good restaurants, shopping, and culture than you can probably fit into a week.

Staying in a hotel in Venice has become very costly. Rooms average more than $200 per night, making Venice unaffordable to many travelers. Timeshare may make a stay in Venice a real possibility for travelers with tight budgets.

RCI has six properties in Venice, and II has three properties. RCI has a spectacular resort located right on the Grand Canal, next to one of Venice's most well-known and expensive hotels.

Most of the timeshares are located on the Lido, a convenient 15-minute water taxi ride away. If you want to swim, the Lido has a good swimming beach and is the perfect location to see the magnificent skyline of one of the world's most beautiful cities.

As with most urban timeshares, you're unlikely to find a large number of two- or three-bedroom timeshare units in Venice (although one II resort only has two-bedroom units — something to keep in mind if you're traveling with family or friends) or timeshare properties with acres and acres of space (no golfing resorts here!).

That said, Venice is a *very* popular tourist destination, with some 23 million visitors recorded every year. Don't expect to trade your timeshare at a moment's notice for a week here. Venice takes some advance planning, but it's well worth the wait.

---

*Mexico Timeshare*

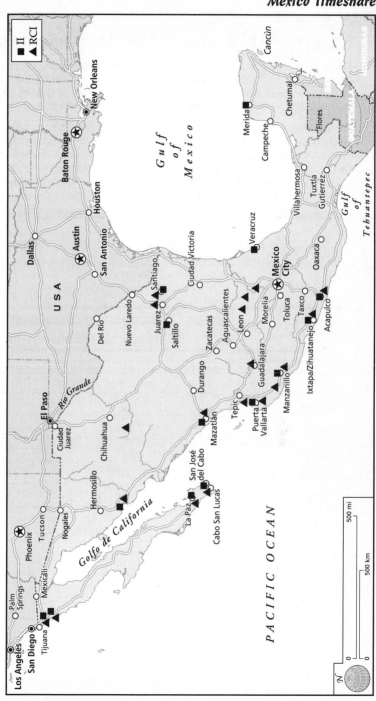

## Snapshot: Fiji, South Pacific, timeshare

You're bored with Orlando and Las Vegas, the Tennessee mountains are just another group of hills, the Grand Canyon is a large hole in the ground, Devon and Cornwall remind you of *Fawlty Towers,* you've bought too many T-shirts in the Caribbean, grabbed enough Mardi Gras beads in New Orleans, and sunk your last birdie in Palm Springs.

Now what? Well, perhaps you should consider Fiji. Yes, Fiji. The remote, exotic island way out there in the Pacific Ocean has timeshare to offer, and superlative timeshare it is. How about a stunning three-bedroom, three-bath suite, where you can rent a car to explore the island, ride bicycles on island trails, rent a sailboat, fish, soak in a hot tub, watch the children play in the outdoor pool, take scuba lessons, and enjoy movies on the VCR at the end of the day. I highly recommend it.

Currently, RCI has 858 Gold Crown Resorts, 666 Resorts of International Distinction, and 292 Hospitality Resorts (for definitions, see Chapter 12). See Table 11-2 for RCI's list of resort locations.

### Table 11-2      Resort Condominiums International (RCI) Resort Locations

| *Northeast United States* | |
| --- | --- |
| Connecticut | 2 |
| Delaware | 2 |
| Maine | 11 |
| Maryland | 14 |
| Massachusetts | 33 |
| New Hampshire | 27 |
| New Jersey | 7 |
| New York | 13 |
| Pennsylvania | 21 |
| Rhode Island | 11 |
| Vermont | 14 |

## Great Britain and Ireland Timeshare

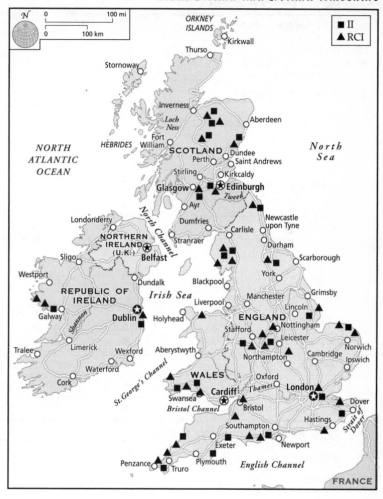

| Southeast United States | |
|---|---|
| Georgia | 18 |
| North Carolina | 48 |
| South Carolina | 92 |

*(continued)*

### Table 11-2 *(continued)*

| *Southeast United States* | |
| --- | --- |
| Virginia | 29 |
| West Virginia | 2 |
| *Florida (United States)* | |
| Central | 58 |
| Eastern | 113 |
| Western | 134 |
| *Gulf States (United States)* | |
| Alabama | 10 |
| Louisiana | 17 |
| Mississippi | 6 |
| Texas | 46 |
| *Mid-South United States* | |
| Arkansas | 14 |
| Kentucky | 3 |
| Missouri | 39 |
| Oklahoma | 1 |
| Tennessee | 24 |
| *Midwest and the Plains (United States)* | |
| Illinois | 1 |
| Indiana | 2 |
| Iowa | 3 |
| Michigan | 14 |
| Minnesota | 12 |
| Ohio | 1 |
| South Dakota | 1 |
| Wisconsin | 30 |

*(continued)*

*Italy Timeshare*

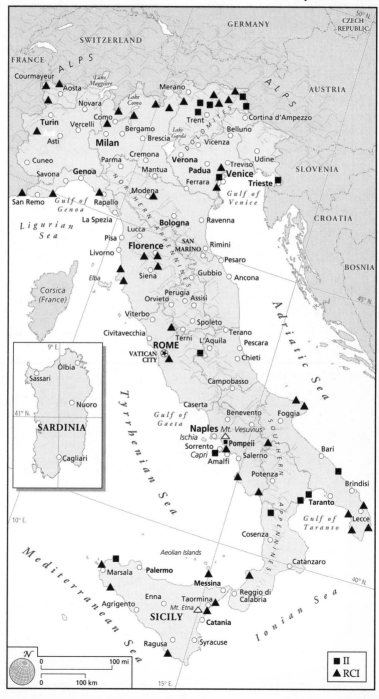

## *Australia Timeshare*

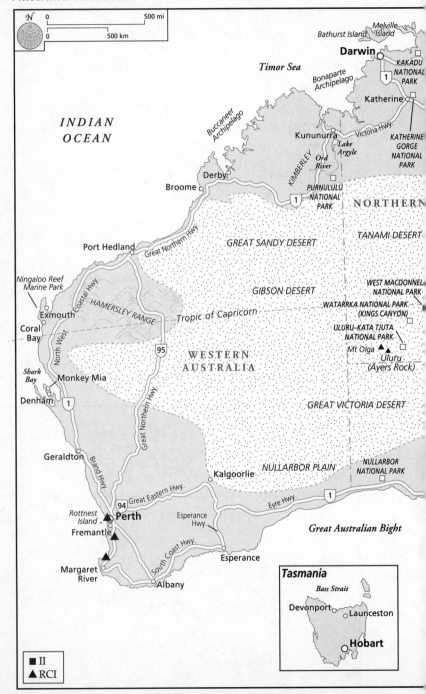

N

| 0 | 500 mi |
| 0 | 500 km |

*Timor Sea*

Bathurst Island

Melville Island

**Darwin**

KAKADU NATIONAL PARK

1

Katherine

Bonaparte Archipelago

*INDIAN OCEAN*

Buccaneer Archipelago

Kununurra

Victoria Hwy.

KATHERINE GORGE NATIONAL PARK

Lake Argyle

Ord River

KIMBERLEY

Derby

Broome

PURNULULU NATIONAL PARK

1

NORTHERN

TANAMI DESERT

Port Hedland

Great Northern Hwy.

*GREAT SANDY DESERT*

Ningaloo Reef Marine Park

HAMERSLEY RANGE

Coastal Hwy.

*GIBSON DESERT*

WEST MACDONNEL NATIONAL PARK

WATARRKA NATIONAL PARK (KINGS CANYON)

Exmouth

North West

Coral Bay

Tropic of Capricorn

ULURU-KATA TJUTA NATIONAL PARK

Mt Olga

Uluru (Ayers Rock)

95

*WESTERN AUSTRALIA*

Shark Bay

Monkey Mia

Denham

1

Great Northern Hwy.

*GREAT VICTORIA DESERT*

Geraldton

Brand Hwy.

Kalgoorlie

*NULLARBOR PLAIN*

NULLARBOR NATIONAL PARK

1

94

Great Eastern Hwy.

Eyre Hwy.

Rottnest Island

**Perth**

Esperance Hwy.

*Great Australian Bight*

Fremantle

South Coast Hwy.

Margaret River

Esperance

Albany

**Tasmania**

*Bass Strait*

Devonport

Launceston

Hobart

■ II
▲ RCI

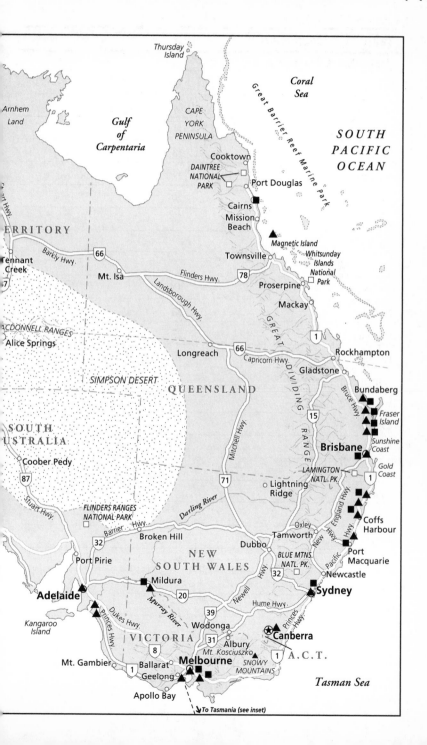

**Table 11-2** *(continued)*

| *Rocky Mountains (United States)* | |
| --- | --- |
| Arizona | 35 |
| Colorado | 64 |
| Idaho | 11 |
| Montana | 13 |
| New Mexico | 19 |
| Utah | 24 |
| Wyoming | 5 |
| *Pacific Coast (United States)* | |
| Alaska | 1 |
| California | 18 |
| Nevada | 33 |
| Oregon | 27 |
| Washington | 20 |
| *Hawaii (United States)* | |
| Hawaii (Big Island) | 18 |
| Kauai | 23 |
| Maui | 19 |
| Oahu | 10 |
| *Canada* | |
| Alberta | 9 |
| British Columbia | 48 |
| Manitoba | 2 |
| Nova Scotia | 1 |
| Ontario | 23 |
| Quebec | 15 |

*(continued)*

## Southern Africa Timeshare

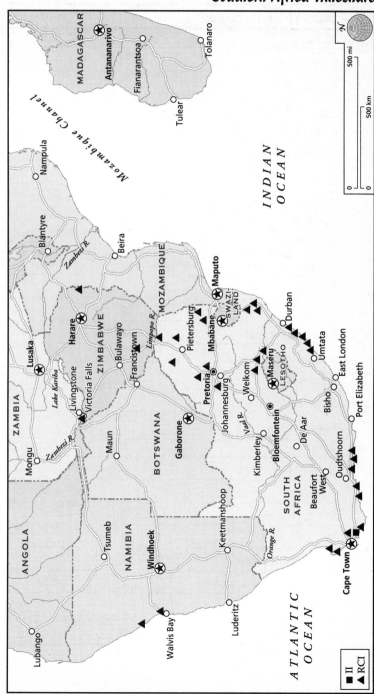

## Table 11-2 *(continued)*

| *Mexico* | |
|---|---|
| Northern/Baja | 46 |
| Northern Mazatlan | 23 |
| Southeast/Cancun | 80 |
| Southwestern | 109 |
| *Bermuda, Bahamas, and the Caribbean* | |
| Antigua and Barbuda | 8 |
| Aruba | 11 |
| Bahamas | 27 |
| Barbados | 10 |
| Belize | 5 |
| Bermuda | 2 |
| Bonaire | 2 |
| British Virgin Islands | 2 |
| Cayman Islands | 5 |
| Curacao | 2 |
| Dominican Republic | 51 |
| Guadeloupe | 9 |
| Jamaica | 8 |
| Martinique | 3 |
| Puerto Rico | 1 |
| St. Kitts and Nevis | 1 |
| St. Lucia | 2 |
| St. Martin/Sint Maarten | 22 |
| St. Vincent and the Grenadines | 4 |
| Trinidad and Tobago | 1 |
| Turks and Caicos | 3 |
| U.S. Virgin Islands | 14 |

| *Central and South America* | |
| --- | --- |
| Argentina | 77 |
| Boliva | 3 |
| Brazil | 84 |
| Chile | 13 |
| Columbia | 29 |
| Costa Rica | 17 |
| Ecuador | 4 |
| El Salvador | 1 |
| Guatemala | 5 |
| Panama | 4 |
| Paraguay | 2 |
| Peru | 2 |
| Uruguay | 26 |
| Venezuela | 49 |
| *Europe* | |
| Andorra | 4 |
| Austria | 19 |
| Belgium | 3 |
| Canary Islands | 102 |
| Channel Islands | 1 |
| Cyprus | 11 |
| Czech Republic | 4 |
| Denmark | 13 |
| England | 172 |
| Finland | 26 |
| France | 66 |
| Germany | 14 |

*(continued)*

## Table 11-2 *(continued)*

| *Europe* | |
|---|---|
| Greece | 35 |
| Hungary | 16 |
| Ireland | 4 |
| Isle of Man | 1 |
| Italy | 150 |
| Malta | 22 |
| Netherlands | 1 |
| Norway | 3 |
| Poland | 1 |
| Portugal | 76 |
| Scotland | 20 |
| Spain | 169 |
| Sweden | 9 |
| Switzerland | 17 |
| Turkey | 27 |
| Wales | 9 |
| *Africa and the Middle East* | |
| Egypt | 53 |
| Israel | 9 |
| Ivory Coast | 1 |
| Jordan | 2 |
| Kenya | 8 |
| Lebanon | 5 |
| Mauritius | 2 |
| Morocco | 6 |
| Mozambique | 1 |

| | |
|---|---|
| **_Africa and the Middle East_** | |
| Namibia | 1 |
| Senegal | 1 |
| South Africa | 162 |
| Syria | 2 |
| Tunisia | 3 |
| United Arab Emirates | 3 |
| Zimbabwe | 6 |
| **_Asia/Pacific_** | |
| Bangladesh | 2 |
| China | 26 |
| Fiji Islands | 7 |
| French Polynesia | 1 |
| India | 59 |
| Indonesia | 30 |
| Japan | 88 |
| Malaysia | 32 |
| Pakistan | 2 |
| Philippines | 19 |
| Saipan | 1 |
| Singapore | 2 |
| South Korea | 17 |
| Sri Lanka | 2 |
| Taiwan | 7 |
| Thailand | 39 |
| **_Australia and New Zealand_** | |
| Australia | 91 |
| New Zealand | 23 |

Currently, II has more than 2,000 resorts worldwide. See Table 11-3 for its locations.

## Table 11-3    Interval International (II) Resort Locations

| *New England (United States)* | |
|---|---|
| Connecticut | 1 |
| Maine | 8 |
| Massachusetts | 24 |
| New Hampshire | 12 |
| Rhode Island | 8 |
| Vermont | 5 |
| *Middle Atlantic (United States)* | |
| Maryland | 8 |
| New Jersey | 6 |
| New York | 4 |
| Pennsylvania | 19 |
| *Southern United States* | |
| Alabama | 3 |
| Arkansas | 8 |
| Georgia | 2 |
| Louisiana | 8 |
| Mississippi | 1 |
| North Carolina | 30 |
| South Carolina | 67 |
| Tennessee | 14 |
| Virginia | 20 |
| West Virginia | 1 |
| *Florida (United States)* | |
| Central | 56 |
| Northeast Atlantic | 21 |

| | |
|---|---|
| *Florida (United States)* | |
| Central Atlantic | 7 |
| Southeast Atlantic | 28 |
| The Keys | 16 |
| Lower Gulf Coast | 11 |
| Sanibel and Captiva | 12 |
| Central Gulf | 7 |
| Upper Gulf | 10 |
| Panhandle | 8 |
| Miscellaneous | 39 |
| *Midwestern United States* | |
| Indiana | 3 |
| Michigan | 8 |
| Minnesota | 7 |
| Missouri | 22 |
| Ohio | 1 |
| Wisconsin | 7 |
| *Southwest and Western United States* | |
| Arizona | 40 |
| Oregon | 17 |
| New Mexico | 2 |
| Texas | 10 |
| Washington | 20 |
| *Rocky Mountains (United States)* | |
| Colorado | 44 |
| Idaho | 8 |
| Lake Tahoe area | 36 |
| Las Vegas | 13 |
| Mesquite area | 6 |

*(continued)*

**Table 11-3** *(continued)*

| Rocky Mountains (United States) | |
|---|---|
| Montana | 7 |
| Reno area | 3 |
| Utah | 21 |
| Wyoming | 2 |
| Miscellaneous | 9 |
| *California (United States)* | |
| Coast | 21 |
| Desert | 21 |
| Mountains | 10 |
| Northern countryside | 1 |
| Southern countryside | 4 |
| Urban | 6 |
| Miscellaneous | 19 |
| *Hawaii (United States)* | |
| Hawaii (Big Island) | 19 |
| Kauai | 16 |
| Maui | 29 |
| Molokai | 1 |
| Oahu | 9 |
| *Canada* | |
| Alberta | 3 |
| British Columbia | 23 |
| Newfoundland | 1 |
| Ontario | 7 |
| Quebec | 3 |

| Caribbean and Atlantic Islands | |
| --- | --- |
| Antigua | 2 |
| Aruba | 15 |
| Bahamas | 6 |
| Barbados | 2 |
| Bonaire | 1 |
| Cancun | 21 |
| Cayman Islands | 21 |
| Curacao | 2 |
| Dominican Republic | 21 |
| Jamaica | 3 |
| Margarita | 8 |
| Puerto Rico | 5 |
| St. John | 1 |
| St. Kitts and Nevis | 1 |
| St. Lucia | 1 |
| St. Martin | 10 |
| St. Thomas | 2 |
| Tortola | 1 |
| Turks and Caicos | 1 |
| **Mexico and Central America** | |
| Belize | 2 |
| Costa Rica | 7 |
| El Salvador | 1 |
| Guatemala | 3 |
| Mexico, Acapulco | 6 |
| Mexico, Baja North | 3 |

*(continued)*

## Table 11-3 (continued)

### Mexico and Central America

| | |
|---|---|
| Mexico, Baja South | 9 |
| Mexico, Chihuahua | 1 |
| Mexico, Ixtapa | 2 |
| Mexico, Mazatlan | 11 |
| Mexico, Nueva Vallerta | 6 |
| Mexico, Puerto Vallarta | 14 |
| Mexico, Saltillo/Santiago | 2 |
| Mexico, San Carlos | 2 |
| Mexico, Taxco | 1 |
| Panama | 3 |
| Miscellaneous | 7 |

### South America

| | |
|---|---|
| Argentina | 39 |
| Bolivia | 4 |
| Brazil | 20 |
| Chile | 5 |
| Columbia | 10 |
| Ecuador | 4 |
| Peru | 1 |
| Uruguay | 7 |
| Venezuela | 6 |

### United Kingdom and Ireland

| | |
|---|---|
| England | 40 |
| Ireland | 4 |
| Scotland | 10 |
| Wales | 4 |

| | |
|---|---|
| ***Canary Islands*** | |
| Fuerteventura | 1 |
| Gran Canaria | 8 |
| Lanzarote | 13 |
| Tenerife | 28 |
| ***Eastern Mediterranean*** | |
| Cyprus | 3 |
| Greece | 9 |
| Turkey | 7 |
| ***Central Europe and the Low Countries*** | |
| Andorra | 2 |
| Austria | 15 |
| Czech Republic | 2 |
| France | 43 |
| Germany | 5 |
| Hungary | 1 |
| Italy | 33 |
| Malta | 7 |
| Portugal/Madeira | 17 |
| Spain | 81 |
| Switzerland | 3 |
| The Netherlands | 1 |
| ***Scandinavia*** | |
| Finland | 17 |
| Norway | 1 |
| Sweden | 1 |

*(continued)*

## Table 11-3 *(continued)*

| *Middle East and Africa* | |
| --- | --- |
| Egypt | 12 |
| The Gambia | 1 |
| Israel | 8 |
| Kenya | 1 |
| Lebanon | 2 |
| Morocco | 4 |
| South Africa | 4 |
| Tunisia | 6 |
| *Australia, New Zealand, and the South Pacific* | |
| Australia | 36 |
| Fiji | 3 |
| New Caledonia | 1 |
| New Zealand | 16 |
| *Asia* | |
| China | 3 |
| India | 1 |
| Indonesia | 3 |
| Malaysia | 10 |
| Nepal | 1 |
| Philippines | 3 |
| Singapore | 1 |
| Thailand | 10 |

# Chapter 12

# Exchanging: Playing the Trading Game

*F*or many people who invest in timeshare, the ability to trade weeks to travel the globe is the biggest selling point. Buying timeshare is a practical way to spend time in different parts of the world without having to break the bank. By exchanging, you can trade your timeshare week for another location and even another week of the year. The ability to do so is influenced by several variables, including the popularity of your own timeshare destination, whether the week you own is in high season or low season, and the quality of your home resort and types of amenities it offers.

Prepare to hear terms like trading power, points-based system, and reservation windows bandied about — all are defined in this chapter. If it sounds confusing, just remember that if you buy a timeshare with good trading power and you have some flexibility in your vacation schedule, you'll do well in the trading game. Keep in mind the following tips:

✔ **Buy in a high-demand destination.** Buying into a resort that's popular with the rest of the world makes it easier to trade for a vacation week in different locations every year.

✔ **Plan as far ahead as possible.** Remember that holidays and summer vacations fill up quickly. Just as you wouldn't call a hotel in New Orleans the day before Mardi Gras and expect to book a room at that time, the same is true of timeshare.

✔ **Be flexible.** Always have two or three resorts in mind and several different arrival times when you make your plans. Make your timeshare reservations first, and then make your travel reservations.

# The Big Two and Other Exchange Companies

In the timeshare exchange game, two companies tower over the rest. The two major exchange companies, *Resorts Condominium International* (better known as *RCI*) and *Interval International* (better known as *II*), represent more than 6,000 resorts around the world. Both companies make money by charging members exchange fees every time they make a trade. Each has its own rating system to determine a resort's trading power.

 The vast majority of timeshares are affiliated with either RCI or II, including most, if not all, of the timeshare purchased from developers in the United States. So if you purchase a timeshare in, say, Gatlinburg, Tennessee, it's pretty much a given that the resort is a member of RCI or II. A number of smaller independents do exist, and I've included their pertinent information in Table 12-1, at the end of this section.

The advantages of dealing with a larger company are obvious: more destinations, more varied and unique choices, and a vastly bigger pool of options. On the other hand, I hear from consumers that the smaller independent companies often provide better and more personal customer service than you get with the large companies. And many RCI customers (and, to a lesser extent, II clientele) are getting tired of being squeezed for more money here and there, hearing "We have nothing to give you on an exchange, but how about trying one of our available getaway or bonus weeks for only $899?" Every few months or so, there's talk of starting a new exchange company, one that promises to correct all the imperfections of the behemoths — but nothing much comes of it.

What is the difference between the two largest exchange companies? Which one is best? There is no "best." Here is a breakdown of each of the big-two exchange companies:

### RCI

| | |
|---|---|
| Total number of resorts | 3,726 |
| Total number of week-based resorts | 3,114 |
| Total number of points-based resorts | 612 |
| Total number of countries served | 100 |
| Types of resorts | |
| Gold Crown | 26% |
| Resort of International Distinction | 24% |
| Hospitality | 10% |
| Standard | 40% |
| Exchange fees | |
| Domestic (U.S. and Canada) | $149 |
| International | $189 per week |
| Major brand names | Starwood, Fairfield, Hilton, Shell |

*Interval International (II)*

| | |
|---|---|
| Total number of resorts | 2,000 |
| Total number of countries served | 80 |
| Types of resorts | |
|     Five-Star | 20% |
|     Standard | 80% |
| Exchange fees | |
|     Domestic (U.S. and Canada) | $129 per week |
|     International | $149 per week |
| Major brand names | Fairfield, Hyatt, Marriott, Westin |

In addition, I am aware of five other, smaller exchange companies: Platinum Interchange, Trading Places International, Hawaii Timeshare Exchange, Donita's Dial Exchange, and San Francisco Exchange. Table 12-1 gives you a breakdown of each, compared with RCI and II statistics. See Appendix A for details on how to reach these exchange companies.

| Table 12-1 | Exchange Companies Comparison Chart | | | | | | |
|---|---|---|---|---|---|---|---|
| | **RCI** | **II** | **Platinum Interchange** | **Trading Places International** | **Hawaii Timeshare Exchange** | **Donita's Dial An Exchange** | **San Francisco Exchange** |
| **Initial membership** | Fee | None | None | None | None | None for basic membership | |
| **Resorts in system** | More than 3,700 | More than 2,000 | More than 700 | More than 500 | More than 300 | | |
| **Exchange fees** | $139 Domestic $179 International Points Fees Range from $17 to $69 | $129 Domestic $149 International | $99 Domestic $119 International | $109–$159 | $69 Internal $89 External | $99 Domestic $125 International | $99–$125 |
| **Annual dues** | $89 for weeks; $99 for points | $79 | None | None | $49 | None | None |
| **Banking options** | Deposit first, request exchange 1 year before or 2 years after date None with points | Request first or deposit first and have a 3-year exchange window | Request first and deposit week when confirmed or bank week for exchange up to 18 months after date of deposited week | Exchange at time of deposit or bank and have 2 year window | Request or bank first, request exchange within 2 years after date of deposit | Deposit upon confirmation or bank for up to 36 months | Deposit or request first (depending on status) or bank and request within 2 years of date of deposit |

| | RCI | II | Platinum Interchange | Trading Places International | Hawaii Timeshare Exchange | Donita's Dial An Exchange | San Francisco Exchange |
|---|---|---|---|---|---|---|---|
| **Upgrades** | Weeks only, subject to availability, based on trading power | All exchanges made less than 60 days have no restrictions | For a fee based on availability | Depending on membership status | Check Web site for availability | Based on availability | Based on availability |
| **Directory** | Large guide with maps, cruises, photos, vacation options, benefits, services, and so on. | Large guide with maps, rules, photos, and so on. | | | | | |
| **Exchanges made (2003)** | More than 2,600,000 | More than 790,000 | More than 26,000 | More than 28,000 | More than 3,000 | Not released | Not released |

# The advent of exchanging

The concept of exchanging or trading your timeshare quickly followed on the heels of the deeded era.

- ✔ **RCI:** The husband-and-wife entrepreneurial team of Christel and Jon DeHaan understood the importance of trading or exchanging individual timeshare weeks, freeing the customer to go anywhere in the world with only one purchase. The idea of exchanging timeshare condos echoed their previous efforts to revive a stagnant RV campground industry by offering exchange memberships to camper owners. In 1974, from the dining-room table in the couple's home, the two created **Resort Condominiums International (RCI)** (www.rci.com), the first timeshare-exchange company. In ten years, RCI sales increased some 10,000%, from $1 million in 1979 to $100 million in 1989. Flash ahead to 1996, when the now-ex–Mrs. DeHaan sold RCI for a cool half-billion dollars, and the Cedant Corporation was born.

  Under Cedant's umbrella, RCI has 3,700 properties, making it one of the two major players in the vacation-exchange field; the other is Interval International (II) (see the following bullet). It's a big umbrella: Also owned by Cedant are **Fairfield Resorts,** the largest vacation ownership company in the world, with more than 450,000 member families; and **Trendwest Resorts, Inc.,** which offers a network of drive-to resorts with a flexible point-based system of ownership. Trendwest currently operates 54 WorldMark vacation club condo resorts in the United States, British Columbia, Mexico, Fiji, and Australia.

  And that's not all. Cendant is also the parent corporation of many companies in the real estate and hospitality industries, among them Century 21, Coldwell Banker, Days Inn, Howard Johnson, Ramada, Super 8, and Travelodge.

- ✔ **II:** The other big leader in timeshare exchange is **Interval International,** simply referred to as **II** (www.intervalworld.com). It was formed in 1976 by Thomas J. Davis, Jr., and Mario Rodriquez, II, as an upscale alternative to RCI. In 2002, II was purchased by what is now InterActiveCorp (IAC), of which the online travel planning site Expedia is a wholly owned subsidiary. II now has some 2,000 resorts all over the world. IAC is headed by former media mogul Barry Diller. The company is another behemoth, this time in travel, shopping, and media. It's the parent company of Expedia, Inc., Hotels.com, TV Travel Shop, Home Shopping Network, and Citysearch.

# The Rules of Exchanging: Determining Trading Power

The two primary exchange companies, RCI and II, derive the majority of their revenues from exchange fees. These companies — not the resort where you own timeshare nor the resort you wish to trade to — are in charge of determining whether you receive your desired exchange. And the bottom line for these companies is maximizing their revenues, not necessarily sending you off on a fun vacation.

In 2003, RCI made approximately 2,600,000 exchanges. At an average exchange rate of $159, that amounts to a whopping $413,400,000. In that same year, II made approximately 790,000 exchanges, which generated about $109,810,000.

So how do these giants generate these numbers? Simple: They look to make trades where the chances of getting two exchange fees are greater.

Both II and RCI use a seven-point evaluation to determine the trading power of your timeshare. But keep in mind that the most important criteria both companies use for insuring a fair trade are supply and demand, and how early your week is deposited.

This comparison is for "traditional" weeks of timeshare, not for RCI's points-based system; see below for more information.

## Point 1: Supply and demand

If you own in a high-demand area, your chances of getting the exchange you want increase. If you own in a location where demand is high but supply is low — Venice, New York City, or Paris, you also have an excellent chance of getting the trade you want. It's all about what you bring to the trading table. For example:

Bob and Vera purchased a two-bedroom timeshare in Branson, Missouri, for $12,000 last year.

Mark and Jan purchased a two-bedroom timeshare in Maui, Hawaii, for $23,000 last year.

Shawn and Amy purchased a two-bedroom timeshare in Orlando, Florida, for $15,000 last year.

This year, independent of one another, all three couples decide to go to Myrtle Beach, South Carolina, during Labor Day week. Assume for a moment that the three timeshares they own are of similar quality (see the "Point 4: Sleeping capacity" section) and that all three couples call at exactly the same time to make the trade. If the resort in Myrtle Beach in question has only one two-bedroom timeshare available for trade during Labor Day weekend, which one of the three couples will get to go?

If you said Mark and Jan, because they paid more, you would have lots of company — but you would be wrong. Shawn and Amy will get their trade. Why? Simple. The money that the couples paid to buy the timeshare went to the timeshare developer. Who is in charge of sending the couples on vacation? The trading company. II and RCI stand to make $129 or $149 from each couple for the trade, but if they can only send one couple to Myrtle Beach, both II and RCI will send the couple that will make the most money for them. A timeshare in Orlando will have more demand from other vacationers than a timeshare in either Branson or Maui — and will likely be snapped up right away.

Even within high-demand areas, there are higher demand times and lower demand times. So even though you purchase your timeshare in a high-demand area, you should also find out what week — or at least season — you are being assigned. Don't leave this to chance; always ask.

## Point 2: Resort location

Timeshare units are not the same from country to country and even state to state. Timeshare resorts located in areas with higher standards of accommodations will give you better trades.

According to II, the top requested destinations in 2003 were Orlando, Florida; Tenerife and Gomera; the California desert; the Yucatan Peninsula, Mexico; and Aruba. Here are the actual numbers:

| Rank | Location | Number of Timeshare Units |
|------|----------|---------------------------|
| 1 | Orlando, Florida | 80,019 |
| 2 | Tenerife and Gomera | 18,703 |
| 3 | California desert | 16,623 |
| 4 | Yucatan Peninsula, Mexico | 14,990 |
| 5 | Aruba | 14,023 |
| 6 | Puerto Vallarta, Mexico | 12,795 |
| 7 | Hilton Head, South Carolina | 11,513 |
| 8 | Spain, southern coast | 9,838 |
| 9 | Lake Tahoe | 9,853 |
| 10 | Broward County, Florida | 9,635 |
| 11 | Maui | 8,775 |
| 12 | Kauai | 8,421 |
| 13 | Lanzarote, Spain | 7,737 |
| 14 | Hawaii (Big Island) | 7,556 |
| 15 | Las Vegas | 7,069 |
| 16 | Vail-Avon-Beaver Creek, Colorado | 6,951 |
| 17 | Florida, northeast coast | 6,564 |
| 18 | Poconos Mountains, Pennsylvania | 6,523 |
| 19 | Arizona (spa destinations) | 6,331 |
| 20 | Austria, mountain areas | 6,288 |
| 21 | California, southern coast | 5,598 |
| 22 | Eastern British Columbia, Canada | 5,302 |
| 23 | Puerto Rico | 5,123 |
| 24 | New Orleans | 5,089 |
| 25 | St. Martin | 5,075 |

## *Point 3: Resort quality*

II has two types of resorts: *Five-Star* and *standard*. RCI has four types of resorts: *Gold Crown, Resort of International Distinction, Hospitality*, and *Standard*. All things being equal, Five-Star and Gold Crown command the most trading power.

The lowest ranking for both companies, Standard, may meet your personal needs just fine. You may find it unnecessary to purchase a higher-priced unit at a higher-rated resort. But keep in mind that your trading power with a Standard unit may be limited; it will likely be diffi-cult to exchange your unit for a high-demand timeshare.

Both trading companies try to give fair trades. If you own in a Five-Star resort (II) or a Gold Crown Resort (RCI), you have the trading power to request *any* resort to trade into, even one of lesser quality. However, if you own a Standard resort, you may only request a resort of the same or lesser quality. You can always trade down, but you cannot trade up.

## *Point 4: Sleeping capacity*

Timeshares typically come as studio, one-bedroom, two-bedroom, or three-bedroom units. A few have four bedrooms or are actual stand-alone houses. Timeshare units with more sleeping capacity typically trade better than units with lesser sleeping capacity.

II and RCI both have a wide variety of timeshare sizes, ranging from studios that sleep two persons to three-bedroom units that sleep ten or more persons. Timeshares with the most *private* sleeping capacity (not necessarily the *total capacity*, which includes sofa beds) are in great demand and will generally give you more trading power.

## *Point 5: Color codes*

All of II's 2,000+ and RCI's 3,726 resorts are assigned a color code to rate the demand at the resorts:

- ✔ II uses a **Red, Yellow, Green** color code, from high demand to low, respectively.

- ✔ RCI uses a **Red, White, Blue** color code, from high demand to low, respectively.

Here's what they mean:

- ✔ Red denotes periods of higher demand.

- ✔ Yellow or White denotes periods of medium demand.

- ✔ Green or Blue denotes periods of lesser demand.

The general rule is if you own in a Red season, you have greater chances of getting your trade most anywhere you want. Resort locations like

Orlando, Florida; Las Vegas, Nevada; and most urban areas (San Francisco and Venice) are all Red, all the time. Some resort areas (like the Pacific Northwest) have certain weeks of the year designated Red (high demand), Yellow or White (middle demand), and Green or Blue (low demand.)

Red weeks are region specific and not universal. The Red weeks in Vail, Colorado, are during the prime ski season. Red weeks in places like Devonshire, England, are during the summer.

Just as with the rankings on resort quality (see the "Point 3: Resort quality" section), with color codes, you can trade down, but not up. If you own in an all-Red area, like San Francisco, you may request a trade to any resort, during any season. However, if you own a timeshare week that has been designated Green or Blue, you may only request a trade to a resort within the Green or Blue weeks, meaning it's unlikely that you will get a trade to San Francisco, which is Red all year long.

## Point 6: Travel Demand Index

To drill down even deeper into the Red, Yellow, and Green system (and to complicate matters), II has come up with the *Travel Demand Index,* which consists of seasonal indexes for each of its 26 regions. Each area in the region is assigned a numerical index for each week of the year, with 100 representing the average travel demand for all regions. The higher the figure, the greater the relative leisure-travel demand for the area during the week. Numbers below 100 indicate periods where the relative inbound leisure-travel demand is lower.

Unlike color codes, which are resort specific, the Travel Demand Index is an analysis of an area's peak season relative to other areas. For example, Orlando, Florida, is Red all year long, as is Maui, Hawaii. Certain weeks in Maui, however, outrate certain weeks in Orlando, according to the Index.

## Point 7: Customer feedback

When you return from a timeshare vacation, RCI mails you a *comment card* (for II it's called an *evaluation form*), which asks you to rate the resort in categories ranging from the service provided by the staff to the quality of accommodations and maintenance. Resorts with consistently positive comment cards maintain higher trading power.

You have to give RCI and II credit for giving so much credence to customer feedback. Both companies place a lot of stock in what owners have to say about their home resort and other resorts in general. Always complete and return the comment card; it's one way for owners to voice their concerns and opinions.

Not only does RCI rely on comment cards to evaluate a resort's trading power, but if a resort consistently receives superior or inferior comments, RCI may revisit that resort to possibly upgrade or downgrade the resort's rating.

## The under-45-day rule

One particularly nice feature for RCI Points Members is the *less-than-45-day rule.* If an RCI Points Member requests an exchange and is confirmed less than 45 days from check-in, he or she needs only 9,000 points to do so, regardless of season or size of unit. Obviously, not everything will be available, but for travelers who have flexibility and like to experience different places and resorts, this is a great feature.

## *Searching for an Exchange Online*

If the thought of thumbing through either of the two big directories of resorts is overwhelming to you, you can find exactly what you're looking for by doing an online search of the resorts. Both RCI and II have very user-friendly Web sites (www.rci.com and www.intervalworld.com) that are continually upgraded.

However, I highly recommend talking to a live person the first time you call to exchange your timeshare, just to make sure you're comfortable with the trade (for example, are you trading half of your two-bedroom, only some of your points, borrowing from next year, using a week that you saved from the previous year?).

### *RCI online*

RCI allows you to do a search based on any number of the following criteria:

- ✔ Gold Crown Resorts
- ✔ Resorts of International Distinction
- ✔ All-inclusive resorts
- ✔ Air-conditioned unit
- ✔ Auto rental facilities
- ✔ Beach
- ✔ Boating
- ✔ Carpet in units
- ✔ Casino
- ✔ Child care
- ✔ Children's pool
- ✔ Conference facilities
- ✔ Cross-country skiing

- ✔ Dishwasher
- ✔ Downhill skiing
- ✔ Elevator
- ✔ Exercise equipment
- ✔ Fireplace
- ✔ Fireplace in unit
- ✔ Fishing
- ✔ Games room
- ✔ Golf
- ✔ Grocery store
- ✔ Hairdresser
- ✔ Handicapped unit
- ✔ Health club
- ✔ Horseback riding
- ✔ Housekeeping
- ✔ Karaoke
- ✔ Kitchen
- ✔ Lake
- ✔ Laundry
- ✔ Live entertainment
- ✔ Medical facilities
- ✔ Microwave
- ✔ Playground area
- ✔ Racquetball
- ✔ Restaurant
- ✔ Sauna
- ✔ Scuba diving
- ✔ Shopping area
- ✔ Ski school
- ✔ Snack bar
- ✔ Spa
- ✔ Special meals (kosher, halal)
- ✔ Squash

- ✔ Swimming pool
- ✔ Telephone
- ✔ Tennis
- ✔ Washer/dryer
- ✔ Water-skiing
- ✔ Whirlpool/hot tub
- ✔ Windsurfing

## *II online*

II's Web site is just as comprehensive, allowing you to pinpoint the resorts that you want using this list:

- ✔ Air-conditioned unit
- ✔ Auto rental
- ✔ Babysitting referral
- ✔ Bar/cocktail lounge
- ✔ Beach
- ✔ Bicycle trails
- ✔ Boat marina/launching
- ✔ Casino gambling
- ✔ Clubhouse
- ✔ Cooking facilities
- ✔ Day spa
- ✔ Entertainment, live
- ✔ Exercise room, equipped
- ✔ Fireplace
- ✔ Fishing
- ✔ Golf
- ✔ Golf program
- ✔ Grocery/convenience store
- ✔ Horseback riding
- ✔ Lake
- ✔ Laundry facilities
- ✔ Lock-off units (units that can be split or locked off into two or more separate units or combined into one large unit)

# ICE, baby: Trading weeks for cruises

**International Cruise & Excursions, Inc. (ICE)** is a leading provider of cruise programs for the leisure industry. ICE's relationships with cruise lines like Carnival, Royal Caribbean, Holland America, and Princess, as well as its partnerships with over 500 international resorts and hotels, enables it to offer customers an array of vacation packages — and allow timeshare owners to exchange weeks for cruises. Call ICE to see how it works (☎ 888-320-4234; www.icegallery.com).

- ✔ Pets allowed
- ✔ Playground
- ✔ Racquetball
- ✔ Restaurant
- ✔ Sailing, rentals
- ✔ Sauna/steam room
- ✔ Size of unit (efficiency/studio, one-, two-, three-, or four-bedroom)
- ✔ Skiing, cross country
- ✔ Skiing, downhill
- ✔ Swimming pool, indoor
- ✔ Swimming pool, outdoor
- ✔ Television, color
- ✔ Tennis
- ✔ VCR or player/video rental
- ✔ Water-skiing
- ✔ Wheelchair accessible

## *The Nitty-Gritty of Exchanging*

In this section, I walk you through the steps of exchanging your timeshare unit with II and RCI.

II uses either the deposit first or the request first methods. RCI uses deposit first and the RCI Points System, wherein the depositing is automatically done for you upon purchasing. These terms are further explained in the following sections.

## Deposit first

Use the *deposit first method* if you're sure you want to exchange your timeshare for time at another timeshare instead of at your home resort.

 If you plan to *deposit* (place your timeshare unit in the trading pool) your week, do so as early as possible. When you deposit your week, what you're doing in effect is giving the exchange company the right to immediately make your week available to someone else. Your chances of getting a fair trade improve the longer in advance you have your week available for use. Some resorts allow owners to deposit as early as two years in advance; other resorts limit you to only one year in advance.

## Request first

Use the *request first method* to check on availability before giving up your rights to your week or if you haven't made up your mind where you want to go on your timeshare week.

 If you own a particularly high-demand week, such as Christmas week in Vail, Colorado; race week in Daytona; or Mardi Gras week in New Orleans, use the request first method. There's no sense giving up such a high-demand week before you know that the exchange company can fulfill your trade. Keep in mind that the exchange companies want your week!

### Floating week versus fixed week

If you own a fixed week, you already know what week you're putting into the system. How do you know which week you're giving up if you own a floating week? Call your resort so it can assign you a week. See Chapter 7 for more on fixed and floating weeks.

### Requesting your exchange

After you know exactly what you have to trade, you can call or go online to request your exchange. Both RCI and II give members an entire directory of all their resorts each year, or you can go get information about other resorts and make the exchange online.

 Be as flexible as you can with your exchange requests. If you want a specific week, select at least three different resorts. If you want a specific resort, select at least three different weeks in order to maximize your chances. You'll receive either confirmation right then and there, or you'll be put on a waiting list.

 The entire exchange system depends on members depositing what they own so that other members have access to them. If you and other owners neglect to deposit your weeks into the system, exchanges will be few and far between.

## The points-based system

One of the major distinctions between RCI and II is the points system, which RCI rolled out in 2000. Currently, approximately 612 of RCI's 3,725 resorts operate on a points system.

Think of points as vacation currency. You can spend your vacation currency for nights at a timeshare or a hotel, cruises, car rentals, airline tickets, just about anything.

Suppose you bought a two-bedroom, two-bath timeshare for $17,000, which gives you 100,000 RCI points annually. You can use your points in a number of ways, including

- ✔ Seven nights at your home resort

- ✔ Two round-trip airline tickets (on selected airlines) within the United States

- ✔ Seven nights at a (select) hotel in Orlando and two adult passes to Universal Studios

- ✔ Seven nights at a nonpoints resort and a one-week full-size car rental

If you own at one of RCI's points-based resorts, you can use your points for time at any of RCI's resorts. And if you choose to go to your or any other points-based resort, you can stay for as few as two nights. Stays at nonpoints resorts are for the traditional seven nights. The RCI directory lists the exact number of points needed to make trades.

With RCI's points, unlike traditional weeks of timeshare, it is not necessary to deposit your timeshare in order to use it. An important point (no pun intended) to remember is that when you buy your timeshare, all your points automatically go into the RCI *points bank,* or pool, for whatever length of time your resort has agreed to be a points resort. On one hand, this system ensures that you can't forget to deposit your week and potentially lose usage, something that can happen with a traditional timeshare. With points, however, there is no such thing as trading power. Points are points are points.

Many RCI week owners report that it is has gotten more and more difficult for them to obtain a good trade lately and fear that RCI is in their words, "saving the good trades for RCI points owners" — in effect forcing them to purchase additional timeshare at a points-based resort.

Although RCI denies this, both RCI and the points-based resorts have much to gain by selling points-based timeshare. The resorts get more dollars by selling more and/or charging to upgrade existing weeks of timeshare to points, and RCI gets more dollars from the associated fees.

If you own a traditional week of timeshare at a resort that is now points-based, the resort cannot automatically change you to points, nor can they force you to change what you own.

## The points system: Pros

Points offer substantially more flexibility. You can stay at some resorts for less than a week, perfect for a driving vacation or Hawaii island-hopping exploration. Points may be saved for up to two years and borrowed from a year ahead, allowing you to customize your vacation. And, in most cases, your points will go further if you stay at nonpoints resorts. Example: 100,000 points will get you either seven nights at Silver Lake Resort (a points-based resort) or two weeks at Orange Lake Resort (a nonpoints resort).

This is a great feature if you're flexible: If you make your resort reservations less than 45 days out, the entire week requires only 9,000 points. In an extreme example, your original $17,000 purchase could get you nine weeks of vacation a year!

## The points system: Cons

Points are not inflation-proof. An airline ticket this year may require 50,000 points. How many points will it require in five years? You simply don't know. And for many people, it can get confusing figuring out how to use points effectively. Should you stay at a points resort or a non-points resort? Use points to cruise or take advantage of a good deal you find in the newspaper?

There are also fees associated with every aspect of point usage. For example, if you use your points to get two airline tickets to Miami, Florida, a three-night stay at a hotel in Miami, a two-night stay at a hotel in Fort Meyers, a two-night stay at a hotel in Key Largo, and a weeklong car rental, you incur six separate fees, ranging from $17 to $69.

Keep in mind that if you want to sell your timeshare, points don't transfer to the new owner.

### Converting your timeshare to points

Converting your timeshare from the week system to a points-based system is both a bone of contention for owners and a possible cash cow for the resorts.

Keep in mind that it is solely up to RCI to determine whether a resort is going to switch to a points-based system. And first and foremost, if the resort where you own switches to points, they can't just switch what you own — you own what you own.

Here's how it works. There is no standard fee that resorts charge to switch to RCI Points. I've heard of resorts that charge up to $4,995 to simply take your week and convert it into X number of points, and offer nothing additional in terms of ownership. That's a lot of money for just a conversion.

# Defending points

"I own eight timeshares, and in my experience, there is both a misunderstanding and a lack of knowledge about points by many owners.

"The key to purchasing a unit that either is in points or can be converted to points is the cost of the unit, plus the cost of the points conversion, along with the number of points you will receive per year. For example, I know someone who sells points resorts for a total of $1,200. Yes, $1,200, and that includes the points system. The number of points is 34,500 per year. Do the math, and you will see that for about $3,600 you can have 103,500 points per year. Yes, you will have three annual maintenance fees, but look how many vacations you can have with that many points! It's the resorts that are charging too much for the conversion, not RCI.

"Unlike trading a week for a week, and being concerned that your non–Gold Crown Resort will not trade for the Gold Crown Resort you want; there is no such concern in the point system. Points are like dollars. If you have enough, you get the resort you want.

"Under the week system, you may have to trade a two-bedroom two-bath unit for a smaller unit due to availability. In other words, you have used up something more valuable to get something worth less. In the points system, you pay fewer points for a smaller unit, or fewer points for a season that's not as desirable. One of the best parts of the points system is that you can arrange a stay for less than a full week. You simply can't do that with the week system. The 45-day, 9,000-point deals that RCI offer are unbelievable. If you can go anytime within the next 45 days, RCI will give you any unit in the inventory for just 9,000 points.

"One problem is that RCI will give away week resorts to points members. Once I called the RCI points department and asked for a unit in Lake Tahoe. No points resorts were available, so they took one from the weeks section. This was a Gold Crown Resort that obviously someone with a week to trade would not be able to trade for. If I were not in the points system, I would have been very upset at this development.

"The cost to convert from the week system to points is another area where complaints are valid. I recently looked at a timeshare at Lake Tahoe. The price was under $4,000. When I asked about converting this to points, I was told by the resort that to do so would cost another $4,000. That unit would have given me about 41,000 points per year. This is outrageous. People who are new to timesharing may not know that this is a rip-off by the resorts."

Jerry Nisker, Orange, California

Other resorts may try to sell you something else in addition to what you own, and then charge little or nothing to switch the whole thing into points. For example, you can buy another week (which is worth X number of points), and they will convert your old ownership for only $199 (or maybe nothing).

Now, if that isn't confusing enough, suppose you own timeshare at a resort that is still on the week system *and* you own a timeshare week in another resort that is on the points system. If so, you can indeed choose to have your week at the nonpoints resort converted into points for that year, and you can do so through the points-based resort where you own. This can be a tremendously flexible feature — you have the best of both — use points when you want them for whatever you want them for, without having to have them every year.

You may hear about *RCI Master Point Brokers,* companies or persons who claim to be able to convert you to points for a fee. Keep in mind that you, the owner, must go through a points-based resort in order to convert to points.

### Points: A tale of three couples

The following three couples want an identical trade:

- ✔ Bob and Vera purchased a two-bedroom timeshare in Branson, Missouri, for $12,000 last year and receive 100,000 RCI points annually.

- ✔ Mark and Jan purchased a two-bedroom timeshare in Maui, Hawaii, for $23,000 last year and receive 93,000 RCI points annually.

- ✔ Shawn and Amy purchased a two-bedroom timeshare in Orlando, Florida, for $15,000 last year and receive 70,000 RCI points annually.

All three couples want to go to Myrtle Beach during Labor Day weekend; it requires 75,000 RCI points to do so. In this case, even though Shawn and Amy own a timeshare in one of the most high-demand destinations

# The early bird

"We have been timesharing for the past ten years and love it. We own two weeks, one in Gatlinburg, Tennessee, and one in Destin, Florida.

"If you plan to exchange your week(s), it is most important to make early deposits in the space bank with your selected exchange company. My two resorts require that maintenance fees be paid for the year that is to be deposited. Therefore, I pay my maintenance fees one year in advance.

"If possible when searching for an exchange, be flexible. The odds of finding the resort or area you want are greater if you search over several weeks or months. The odds are even better if you can travel off-season or at a time many others cannot travel (during the school year, for example). We really prefer traveling to most places in the spring and fall — crowds are much smaller, and you can enjoy the area that much more."

Dianne Loftis, Brentwood, Tennessee

in the world, they don't have enough points to get the trade. If Bob and Vera had requested this trade earlier than Mark and Jan, they would be vacationing in Myrtle Beach, even though their home resort in Branson has lower trading power than either Orlando or Hawaii. With RCI points, timing is crucial.

RCI has certain *reservation windows* during which you must use your points or you lose rights to them. Make sure you know what these reservation windows are, or you may find yourself paying for something after you lost the right to use it.

## *If It's September, It's High Season in . . .*

The color codes that RCI and II use (see the "Point 5: Color codes" section) are general indicators of relative exchange demand. Certain places like Orlando, Florida; Las Vegas, Nevada; San Francisco, California; London, England; Paris, France; the Hawaiian Islands; and Sedona, Arizona, for example, are categorized as "all Red."

But, as anyone who has visited Las Vegas in July when its 115 degrees in the shade or Orlando in the third week of September can tell you, there are different shades of red. That's why it is vital to discover exactly which week you're purchasing even if the resort is designated as all Red, all the time.

Interval International has developed a unique Travel Demand Index that clearly represents a more comprehensive analysis of an *area's* peak season(s) relative to other vacation areas. Note the emphasis of the word "area's" as opposed to "resort's". This Travel Demand Index will be updated at least every two years to account for worldwide travel patterns.

Neither the color code system nor the Travel Demand Index can take into account every conceivable situation. So, although Hawaii's peak demand time is listed as January through August, that certainly doesn't mean that Christmas week is a bad trade. My advice: If you decide a timeshare is right for you, purchase only at a resort in a location where you either:

- ✔ Plan on returning year after year
- ✔ Have evidence that this is a high demand area

Timeshare salespeople got a bad reputation for a reason. Many try to convince you of the worth of something that you cannot check out while at the sales table. If you're looking at a timeshare in Bolivia and you don't plan on returning there often, nor are you sure when Bolivia is in high demand among travelers, don't purchase a timeshare week there, plain and simple!

Table 12-2 gives you an idea of the peak exchange weeks by location.

## Table 12-2    Peak Exchange Weeks by Location

| Area | Peak Exchange Weeks |
|------|--------------------|
| Argentina and Chile, inland | January–early March; December |
| Argentina and Chile, mountains | January–early March; end of June–end of August |
| Argentina, Brazil, and Uruguay, coasts | January–early March; December |
| Arizona and New Mexico, mountains | End of May–August |
| Arizona, desert | January–early May |
| Asia | January–February; end of May–end of August; December |
| Australia, New South Wales, New Zealand | January–March; December |
| Austria, Czech Republic and Hungary | January–early February; end of June–end of August |
| Austria, urban | All year |
| Bolivia, Columbia, Ecuador, Peru, and Venezuela | End of June–end of July |
| Boston | April–September |
| Branson | End of May–September |
| Brazil, inland | January–early March; December |
| California, southern | January–August; December |
| California Bay area | All year |
| California, inland | January–March |
| Californian desert | January–March; December |
| Canada | End of May–August |
| Canary Islands and Madeira | January–March; end of June–end of August; October |
| Caribbean | January–March; end of June–July; December |
| Central America | January–April |
| Central Florida | End of January–end of March; end of June–end of August; last two weeks of December |

*(continued)*

**Table 12-2** *(continued)*

| Area | Peak Exchange Weeks |
| --- | --- |
| Colorado | January–March; end of June–end of August |
| Cyprus and Greece | End of June–August |
| Fiji and New Caledonia | End of June–August |
| Florida, northern coast | End of February–end of April; end of May–end of August |
| Florida, southern coast and Keys | January–August |
| France, general | End of June–August |
| France, mountains | January–March; end of June–end of August |
| France, Paris | All year |
| France, Riveria | April–September |
| Gatlinburg/Pigeon Forge, Tennessee | End of May–August |
| Germany | May–September |
| Great Britian and Ireland | April–September |
| Hawaii | January–August |
| Idaho, Montana, and Wyoming | End of May–August |
| Italy | End of May–August |
| Italy, mountains | January–April; end of June–end of August |
| Italy, urban | All year |
| Lake Tahoe and Reno | End of January–end of March; end of June–end of August |
| Las Vegas | January–June; end of August–end of December |
| London, England | All year |
| Malta | End of June–end of July |
| Mexico | End of January–end of March |
| Mexico, Baja and western | January–April; December |
| Mid-Atlantic | End of May–August |

| Area | Peak Exchange Weeks |
|---|---|
| Middle East | End of June–August |
| Midwest | End of May–August |
| Netherlands and Switzerland | End of June–August |
| New England | End of May–September |
| New Orleans | End of January–end of April |
| North Asia, rural | End of May–August; December |
| Oregon and Washington | End of May–August |
| Portugal and Spain and Andorra | End of June–August |
| Portugal and Spain, coasts | End of June–August |
| Scandinavia and Finland | End of May–August |
| South Africa | January–early March; December |
| South Atlantic, coast | End of May–August |
| Southeast Asia, rural | End of May–August; end of July–end of August; December |
| Southern United States | May–September |
| Texas | End of May–August |
| Turkey | End of May–August |
| Utah | January–March |
| Williamsburg, Virginia | End of May–August |

# Trading: Reading the Fine Print

Both RCI and II strive to accommodate owners' trade or exchange requests based on a *like-for-like* basis. However, it is important to remember that there are almost no hard and fast rules when it comes to trading within either exchange system.

Although trading like-for-like is accepted wisdom in the timeshare world, currently nothing in the RCI or II documentation indicates that you must own Red time in order to get a confirmed trade in another resort's Red time. Nor is there anything prohibiting you from asking for and possibly trading a Hospitality unit for a Gold Crown, or a Standard unit for a Five-Star.

Always read the fine print. For example, in thumbing through the RCI and II directories, you may be tempted to check out other resorts within the same geographic area. In some instances, your timeshare salesperson may even use this as motivation to buy, telling you that you can trade your less costly timeshare for a more expensive timeshare in the same city for just the exchange fee. However, both RCI and II have potential restrictions on exchanging within the same geographic area.

Other factors to consider when exchanging include the following:

✔ Within the RCI Points System, all trades are based on the number of points you have and the number of points you need for a specific reservation. Red, White, Blue, Gold Crown, Resort of International Distinction, Hospitality, and Standard mean nothing in the points system. Trades are made or not made based on the number of points and reservation time: first come, first served.

✔ An owner of a Green Week in a low-demand area should not be able to exchange every year for Christmas week in a 5-Star Resort. Exceptions happen, however. But you do have a higher-percentage chance of getting a Red week if you own a Red week.

✔ If you like a brand's hotels and resorts, you'll probably prefer the brand's timeshares. If you like staying in Hilton properties, you owe it to yourself to check out the Hilton Grand Vacations Club (see Chapter 13). If you love the resorts at Walt Disney World, you owe it to yourself to check out Disney Vacation Club (also in Chapter 13).

✔ Remember that both RCI and II are owned by very large corporations, both of which are in the business of making money. Both companies can and will set aside timeshare weeks to use for their own purposes, which generally means for rental. They make money primarily through exchange fees, so if they have the choice of charging $129 to trade a week or $1,099 to rent a week — well, you see my point here.

RCI makes it clear that member weeks that are deposited for exchange are *not* included in any rental programs. Only member weeks deposited for other services, such as cruises, are included in any rental inventory.

# Chapter 13

# The Brand Names of Timeshare

· · · · · · · · · · · · · · · · · · · · · · · · · · · · · · · · · · · · · · · · · · ·

## In This Chapter

▶ Getting to know the big brands of timeshare
▶ Discovering all-inclusive resorts

· · · · · · · · · · · · · · · · · · · · · · · · · · · · · · · · · · · · · · · · · · ·

*T*he timeshare industry is a vastly different animal than it was even ten years ago. In its efforts to clean itself up and banish the seedier elements, the business attracted the attention of the megabrands of the hospitality business. The brands came to the table in a big way: These days almost two-thirds of new timeshare units are built or managed by the large hotel brands, companies like Disney, Fairfield, Hilton, Hyatt, and Marriott (including the Ritz-Carlton). In getting into the business of timeshare, the brands brought a higher level of service and a quality to the timeshare world. They forced timeshare resorts to be more competitive, a boon to consumers. But they also did a curious thing. They gently nudged the term *timeshare* out of the picture. Very few, if any, call themselves timeshare, as evidenced by Disney, which refers to its product as *Disney Vacation Club,* or DVC for short.

It would be impossible within the confines of this book to give a concise review of all the brand-name timeshares, nor do I have the space to describe the thousands and thousands of non-brand-name timeshares. This chapter offers a brief look at those major companies that most consumers associate with brand-name timeshare — those companies that started in the hotel or motel industry and have since entered the timeshare (er, vacation club) market in a big way.

 Four Seasons, which operates four Private Residence Clubs, asked not to be included in this book, and we are honoring its wishes.

## Bringing in the brands

The industry's attempt to purge itself of the sleaze factor worked in timeshare's favor in one more important aspect: It attracted brand-name hotel and resort companies like Marriott, Hyatt, and Disney, who brought to the industry a level of quality and service — and customer loyalty that relied on both — that forced competitors to work harder to serve the customer, or go bust if they didn't. The result has been a much more concerted emphasis on providing top-notch service and amenities.

*The Wall Street Journal* reports that today almost two-thirds of new timeshare units are built or managed by hotel companies — quite a leap from even ten years ago. The brands do sell product through timeshare presentations, but they more often opt for the softer sell.

The brands offering timeshare and other variations of interval ownership include Disney, Marriott, Starwood, Hilton, Westin, Hyatt, and the Four Seasons.

## *The Pros and Cons of Branded Timeshare*

Brands have been healthy for the timeshare business in general, but I do have one caveat. Here are what I consider to be the pros and cons of the brands in timeshare:

✔ Pros: In most cases, brand-name timeshares offer many perks or values when you use their timeshares and their hotel/motel properties. For example, for every dollar you spend at a Starwood hotel, you may earn points that you can add to the point value of your Starwood timeshare, a plus for both you and Starwood. It's a policy that builds brand loyalty. For more on points, see Chapter 12.

✔ Cons: In most cases, brand-name timeshare is more costly than nonbranded timeshare. However, you are getting more perks, so as the saying goes, you get what you pay for.

Are branded timeshares the way to go? There is little doubt that the introduction of the brand names into the timeshare arena has gone a long way in upgrading the consumer's view of timeshare. The brands have enhanced timeshare's visibility and credibility, because these are names that you know and trust. There's little doubt that if you pay for a Hyatt property, timeshare, or hotel anywhere in the world you know what to expect.

If you're a brand-loyal consumer now, meaning you make an effort to stay at a certain hotel chain when you vacation, it makes good sense at the very least to check out that brand's timeshare program. In particular, the Disney Vacation Club seems to be the timeshare of choice for people who regularly vacation at Disney locations, especially in the Orlando, Florida, location.

Most brand-name timeshares operate in one way or another on a points-based system. The drawback to a points-based timeshare (see Chapter 12) is that, more often than not, no anti-inflation mechanism is built into the systems. For example, your two-bedroom timeshare is worth 100 points every year, and it takes 100 points to trade to another two-bedroom in Vail this year. But that same two-bedroom unit in Vail may require 120 points next year, 135 the following, and so on. Be sure to ask about point inflation and the history of point inflation.

# Brand Names at a Glance

Even among the brands, change is rampant. By the time you read this book, numerous more timeshare resorts may have been gobbled up by a brand name or some brands may have themselves been absorbed into a larger entity. For example, Fairfield and Trendwest are now both owned by Cendant, the parent company of Resort Condominiums International (RCI). Marriott at one point was affiliated with RCI, but has now moved its alliances to Interval International (II).

For now, the following comprise the major brands in timeshare.

## Disney

Disney entered the timeshare (they prefer the term *vacation club*) market in 1991 with the opening of Old Key West at the Walt Disney World Resort. The people at Disney say that their vacation club was created to meet the needs of their guests (Disney does not use the word customer) who indicated that they enjoyed coming back to the Walt Disney World Resort, but wanted more value for their dollar. Research showed that many of these guests wanted to stay on Walt Disney World Resort property, but that staying off property offered them the space they needed. Disney looked at various options and when they added flexibility to the product, the Disney Vacation Club was born.

### Number and location of resorts

Disney Vacation Club currently consists of seven resorts:

- ✔ Disney's Old Key West–Walt Disney World Resort
- ✔ Disney's Boardwalk Villas–Walt Disney World Resort
- ✔ Disney's Beach Club Villas–Walt Disney World Resort
- ✔ The Villas at Disney's Wilderness Lodge–Walt Disney World Resort
- ✔ Disney's Saratoga Springs and Spa–Walt Disney World Resort
- ✔ Disney's Vero Beach Resort–Vero Beach, Florida
- ✔ Disney's Hilton Head Island Resort–Hilton Head Island, South Carolina

### Exchange company used

Disney Vacation Club is affiliated with Interval International. (*Note:* According to Disney, only about 20% of their members exchange or trade to go outside of Disney.)

### Price range

$14,250–$190,000 (average of $17,000–$19,000).

### Type of ownership

Currently, all locations other than Disney's Saratoga Springs and Spa are sold out. Ownership at Saratoga is a 50-year right-to-use, starting in the year 2004. Purchases made in 2005 will be 49-year right-to-use. Although ownership is not deeded in perpetuity, interests may be sold and willed, and all interests are in fact real-estate-interest based.

### What will $15,000 get you?

Disney's basic 150-point package ($14,250) can be used for stays at Disney resorts of as little as one night. High-demand seasons and larger villas require more points. To exchange for a week into a non-Disney, Interval International resort, members require a minimum of 124 points.

Points may be saved or borrowed for one year.

### Pros

The Disney name is the biggest draw. Members know what they're getting and know that Disney is running the show, which provides a certain level of trust and confidence that may be lacking in other timeshares. The sales presentation itself is extremely informative and lacks any hint of high-pressure selling.

### Cons

This is not a program for people who vacation less than one week a year or who aren't already spending $150 per night in a hotel. The annual fees are generally higher at Disney than at other timeshare companies, effectively making the break-even point longer.

## Hilton

Hilton Grand Vacations Company was created in 1992 as a result of a joint venture between Hilton Hotels Corporation and Grand Vacations Limited. Initially, Grand Vacations Limited was a joint venture between the Mariner Group and American Resorts Development Company, which had previously developed 16 vacation ownership resorts throughout Florida.

In 1994, the first Hilton Grand Vacations Club opened in Las Vegas, Nevada, at the Flamingo (adjacent to the world-famous Flamingo Hotel, then managed by Hilton Hotels Corporation).

## Number and location of resorts

Currently, Hilton Grand Vacations Company manages 26 resorts, 8 of which were developed by the company.

Hilton Grand Vacations Company developed resorts include the following:

- ✔ Oahu, Hawaii (2)
- ✔ Las Vegas, Nevada (3)
- ✔ Orlando, Florida (2)
- ✔ Miami Beach, Florida

Hilton Grand Vacations Company managed resorts include the following:

- ✔ Breckenridge, Colorado
- ✔ Island of Hawaii, Hawaii
- ✔ Sanibel Island Florida (5)
- ✔ Captiva Island, Florida (5)
- ✔ Marco Island, Florida (4)
- ✔ Estero Island, Florida
- ✔ Hutchinson Island, Florida

## Exchange company used

Hilton Grand Vacations Club is affiliated with RCI.

## Price range

$14,000–$50,000

## Type of ownership

Deeded real estate interest.

## What will $15,000 get you?

A two-bedroom timeshare in Orlando, Florida. Some options for that usage include

- ✔ One week in that two-bedroom timeshare during the same season
- ✔ Up to 12 days in a one-bedroom timeshare

## Pros

The Hilton brand is one of the most recognized lodging brands in the world today. Hilton manages all its timeshare properties.

Hilton has one of the most user-friendly points-based systems available. For example, all two-bedroom units in the same season are 5,000 points; only the price differs based on location and season. (See the following section for the flip side.)

Gorgeous collateral materials include a quarterly magazine that's informational in nature, focusing on many different vacations, Hilton destinations or not.

### Cons

As with other points-based system, fees are associated with almost every usage.

With as many as five different seasons of timeshare ownership and seven levels of Hilton hotels to use points at, usage with Hilton properties can be a problem if you don't do well with options and choices.

## Hyatt

Hyatt Vacation Ownership opened its first resort in July 1994 at the Hyatt Sunset Harbor in Key West, Florida. Although Hyatt Vacation Ownership, Inc., is a separate company from Hyatt Hotels and Resorts, they are a sisterhood with the same lineage, and they share the benefits, among them the Hyatt Gold Passport Program.

### Number and location of resorts

Currently, Hyatt has 11 timeshare properties located in

- ✓ Sedona, Arizona
- ✓ Carmel, California
- ✓ Breckenridge, Colorado
- ✓ Beaver Creek, Colorado
- ✓ Key West, Florida (3)
- ✓ Naples, Florida
- ✓ Lake Tahoe, Nevada
- ✓ San Antonio, Texas
- ✓ Dorado, Puerto Rico

### Exchange company used

Hyatt Vacation Ownership is affiliated with Interval International.

### Price range

$15,000–$1 million

### Type of ownership

Deeded.

### What will $15,000 get you?

Hyatt Vacation Club chose to not contribute to this section, saying that their price lists are not considered public information.

### Pros

Hyatt does have some locations that offer studio units, which require fewer points to use than the standard one-, two-, and three-bedroom condos, a boon to single travelers or those who don't need a lot of space.

### Cons

As with many branded timeshares, Hyatt operates on a points-based structure, which offers more flexibility in usage but runs the risk of point inflation. In addition, seven distinct timeshare ownership seasons can make matters confusing for those owners who like their usage options simple and clear-cut.

Hyatt Vacation Club provided me with minimal written information and turned down requests for a personal meeting. I wrote this section because I felt strongly that their presence in the timeshare market was worth a mention in this chapter.

## Marriott

In 1984, Marriott became the first branded company within the hospitality industry to enter the timeshare (vacation ownership) industry. They purchased American Resorts with properties on Hilton Head Island, South Carolina.

Since that time, Marriott has broadened its offerings and now has four distinct brands: Horizons by Marriott Vacation Club, their most affordable product line; Marriott Vacation Club International; and two "fractional" property brands (see Chapter 16 for more on fractionals): Marriott Grand Residence Club and The Ritz-Carlton Club.

### Number and location of resorts

The portfolio of resorts current stands at 50, broken down by brands.

Marriott Vacation Club includes the following:

- ✔ Phoenix, Arizona
- ✔ South Lake Tahoe, California
- ✔ Newport Beach, California
- ✔ Palm Desert, California (3)

- Breckenridge, Colorado
- Vail, Colorado
- Fort Lauderdale, Florida
- Miami, Florida
- Orlando, Florida (5)
- Palm Shores Beach, Florida
- Panama City Beach, Florida
- Maui, Hawaii
- Kauai, Hawaii (2)
- Oahu, Hawaii
- Boston, Massachusetts
- Galloway, New Jersey
- Hilton Head Island, South Carolina (8)
- Myrtle Beach, South Carolina
- Park City, Utah (2)
- Williamsburg, Virginia
- Palm Beach, Aruba (2)
- Bailly-Romainvilliers, France (Disneyland Paris)
- Estapona, Spain
- Majorca, Spain
- Marbella, Spain
- Phuket, Thailand

Horizons includes the following:

- Branson, Missouri
- Orlando, Florida

Marriott Grand Residence Club includes the following:

- South Lake Tahoe, California
- London, England

The Ritz-Carlton Club includes the following:

- St. Thomas, USVI
- Jupiter, Florida

- ✔ Bachelor Gulch, Colorado
- ✔ Aspen, Colorado

## Exchange company used

Marriott is affiliated with Interval International (exclusive of the Ritz-Carlton Club).

## Price range

$7,690–$85,000 (exclusive of Marriott Grand Residence Club and The Ritz-Carlton Club).

## Type of ownership

Deeded ownership, with the exception of international and metropolitan locations, which are right-to-use ownership; all have the option to trade for Marriott Rewards points on nonconsecutive years (except The Ritz-Carlton Club). The number of points depends on destination, season value, and villa type and size.

## What will $20,000 get you?

Why $20,000? Well, Marriott declined the $15,000 level and provided information on the $20,000 level.

For a a Platinum season two-bedroom villa in Orlando, Florida, with deeded ownership, you pay $19,200 Additionally, this week has a Marriott Rewards point value of 110,000 that can be traded in nonconsecutive years for hotel stays, airline travel, cruises, or other options.

Points have no expiration date, and members can also earn points by staying at Marriott hotel locations ($1 earns ten points), affinity credit card usage, and the like.

## Pros

Marriott has a 21-day preferential window over other Interval International owners into Marriott resorts, and weeks may be banked for up to two years.

Various levels of Marriott hotel properties are available (TownePlace Suites, Fairfield Inn by Marriott, Residence Inn by Marriott, Marriott, JW Marriott, and Ritz-Carlton).

Also, points may be used for airline tickets, cruises, hotel stays, and other perks.

## Cons

Marriott has a number of fees:

| | |
|---|---|
| Home resort during their week (or season) | $ 0 |
| Other Marriott locations | $79 |
| Out of system | Interval International fees |
| Change week of timeshare to points | $104 |
| Lock-off (two-bedroom to one and one) | $75 |

## Starwood

Starwood Vacation Ownership (SVO) is a subsidiary of Starwood Hotels and Resorts Worldwide, Inc. In 2005, it is celebrating its 25th year as a developer and operator of vacation ownership resorts.

The company is currently developing and operating vacation ownership resorts under the Westin, Sheraton, and St. Regis brands. Through the globalization of the company, owners have access to Starwood's 750+ hotels and resorts around the world.

### Number and location of resorts

The Starwood portfolio of resorts currently stands at 14, broken down as follows:

- ✔ Cave Creek, Arizona
- ✔ Scottsdale, Arizona (2)
- ✔ Nassau, Bahamas
- ✔ Mission Hills, California
- ✔ Avon, Colorado (2)
- ✔ Hutchinson Island, Florida
- ✔ Orlando, Florida (2)
- ✔ Port St. Lucie, Florida
- ✔ St. John, U.S. Virgin Islands
- ✔ Maui, Hawaii
- ✔ Myrtle Beach, South Carolina

### Exchange company used

Some resorts are affiliated with RCI, some are with II, and owners may have the option of dual affiliation.

## Price range

Under $10,000 to over $70,000.

## Type of ownership

Deeded ownership. Different-size units give members different options and Starwood points. *Options* can be used to exchange to different II or RCI locations or to customize stays (for example, less than seven nights) at other Starwood Vacation Ownership properties. *Starwood points* can be used for nights at the Starwood family of hotels. Note that members can only convert their ownership to Starwood points every other year, unless they own enough timeshare to qualify for *elite status,* which in most cases is two weeks of timeshare.

## What will $15,000 get you?

A two-bedroom in Orlando will get you 95,700 options or 56,000 Starwood points at a cost of approximately $26,900. The same number of options or points may cost substantially more or less at other locations, such as Hawaii.

Weeks may be banked for up to two years. Also, points have no expiration date, and members can also earn points by staying at Starwood hotel locations ($1 earns points) or using an affinity credit card. Points can be used for airlines, cruises, and other perks.

## Pros

Starwood pros include no blackout dates, and no fee to trade into other Starwood Vacation Ownership resorts.

Resorts are not capacity controlled. *Capacity control* is a system that many hotels, cruise lines, and airlines use to restrict usage. It's akin to trying to use frequent-flier miles for a flight. The airline allows only x number of seats per flight to be used for frequent flier miles or even for persons with discounts. The plane may have unsold seats remaining, but if the airline has filled its quota of frequent-flier seats, that's that. Because the Starwood system is not capacity controlled, if you have the required number of points (or options, whichever) and any room is available, they will give it to you, as opposed to holding the room for someone who is paying the full rate.

As with other brand names, points may be used for airlines and cruises, as well as stays at the various Starwood hotels (Sheraton Four Points, Sheraton, Westin, W Hotels, St. Regis, and The Luxury Collection).

### Cons

Starwood's system can be quite confusing to untangle, for example, the difference between options, points, weeks, and the corresponding rules that apply to each of them.

# All About All-Inclusive Resorts

An increasingly popular option is all-inclusive vacations, and timeshare resorts around the world — including those operated by the big brands — are making this available to vacationers.

What is an *all-inclusive* timeshare vacation? All-inclusive plans have fees that are over and above the normal exchange or trading fee that II and RCI charge (currently $129–$189 per week). Although all-inclusive plans vary from resort to resort, the packages typically cover:

✔ **All meals for the week:** Breakfast, lunch, and dinner with varying cuisines.

✔ **Refreshments and beverages:** Although some may not include alcoholic beverages.

✔ **Resort activities and entertainment:** Traditional dances may be featured one night after dinner in Mexico, for example, while arts-and-crafts lessons may be available in Panama.

✔ **Sports and recreation equipment:** Options may range from basic beach volleyball to kayaks, snorkeling, and even scuba.

Before booking your vacation, contact the resort or your II or RCI representative to find out what exactly is included in the package. You may want to book only the meal package, for example, and not the entertainment and activities package.

In addition, as you can see from the following list, some resorts are *mandatory all-inclusive* while others are *optional.* Many of RCI's Mexican resorts are mandatory all-inclusive. This is not a bad thing, but always ask before you go, so that you know you're responsible for paying all-inclusive fees. RCI offers all-inclusive resorts in the following destinations:

### Optional Locations

| | |
|---|---|
| Bermuda, Bahamas, and Caribbean | 24 |
| Europe | 1 |
| United States Pacific Coast | 2 |
| Central and South America | 14 |
| Africa and the Middle East | 1 |
| Mexico | 20 |

### *Mandatory Locations*

| | |
|---|---|
| Bermuda, Bahamas, and Caribbean | 41 |
| Central and South America | 14 |
| Europe | 2 |
| Canada | 3 |
| Portugal, Spain, and the Canary Islands | 4 |
| Africa and the Middle East | 1 |
| Mexico | 51 |
| Asia/Pacific | 1 |

# Part IV
# Using Your Timeshare

The 5th Wave    By Rich Tennant

"Can you explain your rental program again, this time without using the phrase, 'yada, yada, yada'?"

# In this part . . .

**T**imeshare is used in many different ways: as a home resort, as an exchange property, and even as a rental property. In this part, I discuss how to get the most out of your timeshare week; the questions to ask to ensure that the timeshare resort you're buying into has the service, quality, and amenities you need; and how to go about renting, selling, or willing your timeshare. I also discuss timeshare beyond timeshare: vacation clubs, urban interval ownership, fractionals and condo hotels, and private residence clubs.

# Chapter 14

# Getting to Know Your Resort

. . . . . . . . . . . . . . . . . . . . . . . . . . . . . . . . . . . . . . . . . . . .

## In This Chapter

▶ Finding out more about your home resort
▶ Arriving and checking out your resort
▶ Helping rate the resorts
▶ Packing for your timeshare vacation

. . . . . . . . . . . . . . . . . . . . . . . . . . . . . . . . . . . . . . . . . . . .

*M*any consumers are perfectly happy purchasing and using one timeshare resort (the so-called *home resort*) year after year. Unlike consumers who invest in a resort with the express purpose of exchanging it for timeshare weeks at other resorts (see Chapter 12), people who visit their home resort every year are there because they're satisfied with the location and happy with the resort and its amenities.

Even if you're purchasing your timeshare with the express interest of trading (exchanging) it, always buy with quality and value in mind. Remember, if you're not comfortable there, chances are other people won't be as well, and your trading power will decrease.

This book has a lot of information on how to look for, buy, finance, and exchange your timeshare. But what happens when you're ready to actually *use* your timeshare? In this chapter, I address those aspects of a timeshare resort that mean the most to owners — whether it be 24-hour concierge, maid service, fast maintenance responses, proximity to amenities and services, or all the above. I discuss those things that the most well-run resorts — both home resorts and exchanges — do that keep timeshare owners happy and coming back year after year.

## Checking In — and Checking It All Out

You can tell a lot about a resort from the little details. A rusty tub here, fresh flowers at the front desk there; grit and sand on the kitchen floor versus a lightning-fast response to a maintenance request. In the hospitality business, location and setting are important, but for many people,

# Before you buy: Asking the right questions about your resort's amenities

You've toured the resort and the unit available for purchase, and you and your family are smitten. You can easily see yourself spending happy vacations here every year. You've asked all the major questions (see Chapter 7) about purchasing timeshare in general. Here is a list of questions and concerns you should ask about your home resort's amenities:

- ✔ **Do I have day privileges here?** In other words, suppose you purchase a one-bedroom timeshare in Newport Beach, California, and live in Long Beach, California. Do you have the right to use the resort's amenities if you're not staying on property?

- ✔ **Does the resort have a home owners' association (HOA)?** How are owners kept apprised of what is going on at the resort? In my opinion, you should never purchase at a resort where owners aren't members of the homeowners' association; otherwise, owners have little say in the daily operations and maintenance of the resort. For more on HOAs, see Chapter 7.

- ✔ **What are the exact names and phone numbers of the people at the resort that I need to contact in order to . . .**

    . . . make a reservation at that resort

    . . . get a week assigned (if you own a floating or flex week)

    . . . ask questions about mortgage payments

    . . . ask questions about maintenance and real estate taxes

    . . . refer friends, family, and co-workers to the resort

- ✔ **Does the resort offer discounts on area attractions, restaurants, and so on?**

- ✔ **Are there discounts for food, drinks, and shopping for owners and if so, what are they?**

- ✔ **Do owners need an identification card in order to enter the resort or use the resort amenities? How do I obtain one?**

- ✔ **Do guests need identification cards and how do they obtain them?**

- ✔ **Are there reciprocal privileges at other resorts owned by the same company in other locations?**

- ✔ **What discounts are offered for other services?** For example, if you purchase at an RCI-affiliated resort, do you or can you obtain discounts for Holiday Inns? If you purchase at an II–affiliated resort, do you or can you obtain discounts or special offers from Expedia?

service is the deal-breaker. In fact, service is one of the features that both RCI and II (the two leading exchange companies — see Chapter 12) rely on when rating resorts. So, in this section, I give advice on what to expect at check-in and how to ensure that you get the timeshare vacation you want.

You can get a great deal of information on a timeshare unit in the RCI and II directories of resorts. For every member resort, their catalogs list both the resort's on-site amenities — from swimming pools to restaurants to laundries — and its unit amenities, like fireplaces, microwaves, dishwashers, hair dryers, and washer/dryers. It describes the unit type (two-bedroom, for example) and potential occupancy. It also says whether a unit is wheelchair-accessible or pet-friendly.

## Checking out check-in

Remember to check the check-in days. Most timeshare resorts limit check-ins to certain dates: generally Fridays, Saturdays, and/or Sundays. Most resorts that operate on a points-based system allow check-in every day of the week, but call ahead to confirm.

If you're using the timeshare on an exchange, bring a printed confirmation of your exchange. In the best situation, you'll never need it, and in the worst situation, you have it as backup. Always carry your RCI, II, or other membership card.

Call or e-mail the resort before you travel to find out what supplies are already in the room. Most timeshares come equipped with starter packages: a roll of paper towels, a small supply of coffee filters and instant coffee, and a small supply of dishwashing detergent and laundry detergent. If you're checking in to a resort that doesn't offer this service, remember to indicate it on the comment card; service counts!

It is during check-in that you will invariably be asked whether you would like to schedule an _informational breakfast_ or your _resort update._ These are all polite terms for a timeshare sales presentation to determine whether you want to purchase another week or two of timeshare. My advice: Don't book anything when you check in. Take a few days to decide for yourself whether you want more information. Remember, attending a timeshare sales presentation in this scenario is absolutely optional. This caution about "informational breakfasts" or "resort updates" is not to be taken as an anti in-house sales department stance. I worked very happily in an in-house timeshare sales department for nine months and had some very satisfied clients who went on to purchase another week or two of timeshare. I simply suggest that you take a few days to acclimate yourself with the resort.

Most resorts have a check-in time of 3 p.m. or 4 p.m., which more often than not means you'll arrive earlier than that and not have a room to check into. When you make your call to the resort just before leaving home, be sure to ask whether the resort has a secured, locked area where you can stash your luggage prior to checking in. A topnotch resort will even have your bags taken to your room for you while you're out swimming, seeing the sights, or dining.

Get a parking sticker or some form of vehicle identification for each vehicle you're using. If the resort has a security person at the front gate (and good resorts do), make it a point to introduce yourself and everyone in your party. And if you're traveling with one or more people, get at least two room keys — and ask whether the resort charges a fee for lost keys (they shouldn't).

As a safety precaution, I often test resort staff for potential security lapses. I tell him or her that I lost my room key and request another. If the clerk does not ask for some identification and merely hands over another key, I discreetly alert the manager.

## *Checking out your room*

When you get to your room or villa, the first thing to do is make sure it's the right one. If you booked a full two-bedroom, two-bath, you shouldn't be in a one-bedroom with an attached studio. Alternatively, if you traded for a one-bedroom and find yourself in a two- or three-bedroom, you may want to find out why. Then again, maybe you don't!

Both the RCI and II directories clearly show the types of accommodations that are available. In some lucky instances, you may even get more than you traded for. For example, I once traded a third of my three-bedroom unit in Orlando (a one-bedroom) and received a two-bedroom unit in Venice, Italy. Because the Venice timeshare had no one-bedrooms, I was able to upgrade at no additional charge.

Some slightly confused owners fail to correctly "split" their timeshare and lose a full week. If you own a two-bedroom that splits into two separate one-bedrooms, make certain when you book that you are only using a one-bedroom if that is what you want in return, and are saving the other one-bedroom for another week. Too often, owners simply call to make an exchange without thinking of the type of trading power they own and what they can exchange it for.

Almost all timeshare units have a kitchen or an efficiency kitchen, usually with a checklist posted of the kitchen inventory. Make sure that everything on the checklist is accounted for and report any discrepancies to the front desk. If the unit doesn't have a checklist, have the front desk get one to you within an hour so that you can make sure everything is in order. You don't want to be charged extra for "four sets of silverware" — inventory you never saw in the first place — when you check out.

Check the linen and towel supply and find out what the policy is for getting fresh linens and towels (especially if you don't want to do laundry on your vacation). Ask about the fee (if any) for laundering linens and towels. Also be sure to find out whether the pool and/or spa have different towels available.

# Beefing up quality control

Tighter government regulations and reliable service from the major brands have undoubtedly helped to raise the quality of timeshare product. So do annual rankings and ratings — both within and outside the industry. Both RCI and II award resorts that consistently exceed the company standards of product quality, service delivery, and customer satisfaction. The top designation for RCI resorts is the RCI Gold Crown; for II it's Five-Star. These awards are deemed the highest level of excellence in resort accommodations and hospitality. These resorts have a level of amenities rarely seen in the early days of timesharing, offering such on-site extras as spa services, fireplaces, DVD/CD players, valet parking, and more. For specifics on RCI and II rankings, go to Chapter 12.

In addition, independent timeshare organizations, like the online Timeshare Users Group (TUG) (www.tug.com), not only help consumers stay informed but also give annual awards to those timeshare resorts with consistently excellent product and service; for a list of the latest winners, flip to Chapter 1.

Independent consumer watchdog groups such as TUG also work to offer detailed descriptions — and gloves-off critiques — of timeshare resorts, a grass-roots effort aimed at keeping the industry on top of any problems or issues and ensuring that consumers have the best possible timeshare experience.

Also check the water pressure in the sink(s) and bathtub(s). Take a look, too, at all the lights (ceiling, tables, floor, refrigerator). Call maintenance or go directly to the front desk to report that something isn't working properly. If repairs can't be made before nightfall, ask to be moved to another room — any respectable resort will be happy to accommodate you.

Be sure to determine what the fees are for using the telephone and/or Internet. More and more resorts (as well as hotels) are imposing a hefty charge for toll-free and/or local calls. Ask before you dial.

It's also a good idea to ask the following questions:

✔ What are the hours of the front desk?

✔ Who do you call with a maintenance issue, and is maintenance available 24 hours a day?

✔ Is there a resort concierge? If so, it's a good idea to introduce yourself and see what services he or she provides.

✔ Is there a restaurant on property? What are the hours? Do they have room service? Is it complimentary? Can you get items to go?

✔ Where are the vending machines?

- ✔ Where are the laundry facilities (if you have a room without a washer and dryer)? Are there certain times of the day when you cannot use the facilities?

- ✔ Where is the ice machine (if you have a refrigerator without ice-making capabilities)?

- ✔ Does the resort have movies for rent? Where can you rent them? What are the fees and terms?

# Rating the Resorts: Member Comment Cards

As the quality of timeshare has gone up, so have its service expectations. A resort can be set in a dreamy location, offer topflight amenities, and boast stellar views, but if check-in takes forever, no one is around to fix the air-conditioner, the bathroom is dirty, and the ceiling leaking, the whole vacation experience can be a wash. These are the kind of quality-of-life timeshare issues that can make the difference in a top-rated timeshare resort and an also-ran.

To develop their own internal ratings systems, both RCI and II rely heavily on member *comment cards* (in II's case, they're referred to as *evaluation forms*), wherein resorts are rated by timeshare users. This is one feature of timesharing that owners say puts it above the hotel/motel experience. While hotels and motels are generally rated by AAA or other organization, timeshares are rated by the people who use them. I urge you to fill out these cards — their significance in helping the resort and exchange companies rate member resorts cannot be overstated.

The comment cards and evaluation forms ask owners and exchangers to rate the different aspects of their vacations, from the overall quality of the resort to the specifics: Was the unit ready at the scheduled time? Was the staff responsive to your needs? How clean was the unit? What was the condition of the furnishings? The RCI and II resort ratings described in the following section are based on both RCI comment cards and an evaluation of resort facilities, amenities, and services.

Although one overriding feature doesn't set an RCI Gold Crown above an RCI Resort of International Distinction, for example, ratings for resorts can and do change. Always check the latest RCI and II directories or go online to ensure that the Five-Star resort you're thinking of buying is in fact still a Five-Star.

## Rating the resorts: RCI

RCI has four internal resort ratings in their network:

### RCI Gold Crown criteria

A select number of RCI resorts — judged by the most stringent standards in the industry — are recognized as *RCI Gold Crown Resorts*. These resorts have attained the highest level of excellence for resort accommodations and hospitality.

Each resort receiving the RCI Gold Crown Resort designation has met quality and service requirements based on both RCI Member Comment Card ratings and an evaluation of resort facilities, amenities, and services.

Recipients of this award for superior quality and exceptional service have also met standards in five RCI member comment card categories and each resort facilities category in the evaluation. Performances in each of the comment card categories is compiled over a 12-month period. Resorts meeting these standards then undergo a facilities evaluation.

RCI member comment card criteria for a Gold Crown Resort includes the following:

- ✔ Check in/check out
- ✔ Hospitality
- ✔ Resort maintenance
- ✔ Unit maintenance
- ✔ Unit housekeeping

Resort facilities criteria for a Gold Crown Resort includes the following:

- ✔ Resort amenities
- ✔ Guest services
- ✔ Unit amenities/interiors
- ✔ Resort maintenance

## RCI Resort of International Distinction criteria

Resorts that have achieved excellence in providing outstanding vacation experiences for RCI exchange guests receive the *RCI Resort of International Distinction* award. Each resort receiving this designation has met exacting quality and service standards. Selection is based on ratings from RCI member comment cards submitted by members after their vacations. Resorts receiving the RCI Resort of International Distinction award have demonstrated a consistent, impressive record of satisfying RCI guests and have met requirements in each of five categories of evaluation. Performance data in each of these categories is compiled over a 12-month period for each affiliated resort to determine eligibility for this award.

RCI member comment card criteria for a Resort of International Distinction includes the following:

- ✔ Check in/check out
- ✔ Hospitality

- ✔ Resort maintenance
- ✔ Unit maintenance
- ✔ Unit housekeeping

## RCI Hospitality criteria

Resorts that consistently deliver outstanding customer service and hospitality to exchange guests receive the RCI Hospitality award.

Resorts achieving this designation have received consistently high scores in two categories. (Resorts receiving RCI Gold Crown or RCI Resort of International Distinction are not eligible for this award.) Performance data in the two categories is compiled over a 12-month period for each affiliated resort to determine eligibility for this award.

RCI member comment card criteria for an RCI Hospitality Resort includes the following:

- ✔ Check in/check out
- ✔ Hospitality

## Miscellaneous RCI criteria

In addition to the all-important comment cards, RCI has some fairly strict criteria that a resort must match to even be included on its roster of resorts.

RCI has a listing of 9 *required amenities* and 26 *additional amenities* that resorts are required to meet (either with two of the required and three of the additional or one of the required and six of the additional).

 Required amenities include such offerings as an on-site pool, a minimum of ten tennis -courts, a national theme park within 10 miles, and an ocean beach within a mile.

Additional amenities include such niceties as a whirlpool or hot tub on-site, restaurants within a mile, an on-site recreational center, a historic site within 10 miles, and horseback riding within 5 miles.

When evaluating the actual rooms, RCI has even stricter requirements, ranging from alarm clocks and clock radios to hair dryers, washer and dryer, food processors, wet bar, room service, and can openers.

In the area of guest services, all resorts must offer all the following:

- ✔ In-room area information booklet
- ✔ 24-hour-a-day nonmedical emergency service
- ✔ On-site front desk a minimum of eight hours a day

> 🗸 On-site laundry facility/service
>
> 🗸 On-site maintenance a minimum of eight hours a day
>
> 🗸 Complimentary midweek housecleaning (unless the resort supplies full cleaning amenities)

## Rating the resorts: II

II has two types of internal resort ratings for its resorts. They include:

> 🗸 Five-Star (the top rating)
>
> 🗸 Standard

II measures the standards of its member resorts by reviewing the evaluation forms completed by exchange guests, conducting resort inspections, and using its own quality rating system. The quality rating system weighs such criteria as

> 🗸 The desirability of a particular resort
>
> 🗸 The actual unit
>
> 🗸 The destination
>
> 🗸 The physical properties of the resort
>
> 🗸 The quality of services and amenities

# Packing for a Timeshare Vacation

Your home away from home won't be complete without your stuff — all of life's little necessities that you take for granted in your own home.

Many resorts offer small starter packages of kitchen and bathroom supplies, and many resorts also offer convenience stores that sell basic supplies and food. Expect to pay a little more for convenience-store items, as opposed to buying in bulk at your local chain or home center. Towels, linens, serving wear (plates, glasses, cutlery), cooking pots and pans, small appliances, TV/VCR/DVD, CD player, microwave, washer/dryer, dishwasher, telephones, hair dryers, dataports, alarm clocks, and irons and ironing boards are supplied in most timeshare resort units. But always find out exactly what's offered (and what you need to bring with you) before you go. Of course, in addition to the suggestions in the following list, you may want to include other essential items that you can't live without for a week.

> 🗸 **Your RCI or II membership card and your confirmation from RCI or II:** You need to present your membership card when you check in, and it's always smart to have your confirmation on hand in the (unlikely) event that your reservation is lost.

✔ **Kitchen/laundry supplies:** Laundry detergent, fabric softener, dishwashing liquid, dishwasher detergent, kitchen sponge or dishwashing brush, general cleaning solutions, coffee filters and coffee, paper towels, and oven mitt.

✔ **Cooking supplies:** Salt, pepper, and any other spices you expect to use; ketchup, mustard, mayonnaise, and any condiments you expect to use; aluminum foil, plastic baggies, garbage bags; plastic containers; and flour, sugar, and basic nonperishable foodstuffs you plan to cook with (pasta and rice, canned soups, canned tuna, cooking oils, vinegar, and the like).

✔ **Bathroom supplies:** Toilet paper, tissues, soap, and shampoo.

✔ **Paper goods:** Paper plates, napkins, and cutlery for those days you don't want to wash dishes.

✔ **Prescription medicines and over-the-counter medicines:** First-aid kit, aspirin, Q-tips, band-aids, antibacterial cream, and sunscreen.

✔ **Entertainment:** Music CDs or tapes and/or videotapes, DVDs, books, magazines, card games, tennis rackets, golf clubs, swimsuits, and other sports equipment.

✔ **Miscellaneous:** Candles/candle holders, light bulbs, corkscrew, cocktail napkins, stamps, scissors, small sewing kit, good paring knife, umbrella, beach towels, and a cooler.

# Chapter 15

# Renting, Selling, or Willing Your Timeshare

*In This Chapter*

▶ Using your timeshare as rental property

▶ Putting your timeshare on the market

▶ Willing your timeshare to family or friends

*Y*ou may have purchased a perfectly good timeshare in a perfectly good location for a perfectly good reason — but you can't use it this year or you simply aren't interested in keeping it. What are your options?

Your timeshare salesperson, sales manager, and deeder should have the answers to any and all of your timeshare usage questions, including whether you can rent out your timeshare, what you need to do if you want to sell the timeshare, and what happens if you choose to will your timeshare.

## Renting Your Timeshare

If you're unable to use your timeshare in the short term, consider turning it into rental property until you're ready to use it yourself.

Renting a timeshare is a good option for people who don't own timeshare but may be interested in purchasing somewhere down the line. Renting a fully equipped condo (with kitchen facilities) also makes economic sense for families who don't want to spend money on multiple hotel rooms and who want to save money on dining out.

Before you buy timeshare, ask about the rental options, just in case. Ask the salesperson:

> ✔ Can I rent the timeshare out if I don't want to or can't use it?
>
> ✔ Can I exchange my timeshare for somewhere else and rent it to anyone at any place if I don't want to or can't use it?
>
> ✔ Can a two-bedroom timeshare be used for two separate weeks in a one-bedroom timeshare?

## *Getting compensated for your rental*

Say you've bought a timeshare, and you are allowed to use it as rental property. What can you expect to charge for the rental? Timeshare rental prices vary widely, depending on such variables as location, demand, season, quality of resort, on-site amenities, unit size, and in-room amenities. If you own a top-rated timeshare in a high-demand location in a high-season resort, you can easily command top prices (and even make money in the process — savvy owners know that with the right variables, this is a distinct possibility).

When computing the cost of your rental, consider the cost of your timeshare and its relation to the cost of a standard hotel room in your location. So, for example, here is the cost of an average two-bedroom timeshare, with average monthly payments:

| | |
|---|---|
| Purchase price | $13,500 |
| Down payment | $1,350 |
| Amount financed | $12,150 |
| Monthly payment | $240.63 (15.9% for 7 years) |

If you multiply that $240.63 monthly payment by 12, you're paying $2,887.56 per year plus your annual maintenance fees and/or taxes. Break that down further per bedroom-week ($2,887.56 divided by 2 weeks = $1,443.78 per week), divide by 7, and the per-night cost of your timeshare is $206.25.

Location and demand are key factors in rental income. Suppose you own a timeshare in a prime location in Hawaii, where you can expect to pay at least $200 a night for a typical hotel room. So it makes sense to charge that much (or more) to rent out a complete one-bedroom condo.

If, however, you own timeshare in rural Louisiana, where it's reasonable to expect that a hotel room costs much less than that in a prime location in Hawaii, you may not be able to charge your per-night cost of roughly $200 for your timeshare. On the other hand, you may find that any income you can make on timeshare you're not using is worth the rental.

## *Finding renters*

How do you find renters for your timeshare? It's easy.

✔ **Advertisements:** A quick glance on eBay (www.ebay.com) and Craig's List (www.craigslist.org) gives you an idea of how simple this is. *TimeSharing Today* (www.tstoday.com) is another good place to advertise weeks that you can't use. Local newspapers and even flyers posted on a bulletin board at work or at a local grocery store also work well. Remember that you're simply providing people with an alternative to a hotel.

Use the resources of the timeshare resort you purchased from. Many timeshare resorts have rental programs that rent out your time at the resort if you aren't able to use it. Be sure to ask about the fees (you will almost always have to pay a fee to the resort to rent out your timeshare) before you sign away your rights for that week.

✔ **Word of mouth:** This is the simplest and, in my opinion, best way of renting your timeshare.

Suppose you can't use your timeshare week this year. Coincidentally, your good friends Toni and Allen say they are thinking of going to Branson, Missouri, around the same time for a vacation. Toni and Allen have looked into hotels and express concern that the cost for the hotel room alone averages $150 a night.

You own a one-bedroom condo just off the main strip with a full kitchen, a Jacuzzi, three swimming pools, and a miniature golf course. You offer it to your friends for $150 a night, the same price they would pay for a hotel room, but with complete cooking facilities and top-rate amenities.

In the transaction, you make $1,050 for renting your condo, perhaps leaving you with around $400 that you paid for that year but didn't get compensated for. Your friends get a nice condo at a place that they wanted to go to anyway. You've provided a service, gotten something for your unused time, and everyone wins.

Toni and Allen are not required to attend any type of timeshare presentation when they stay at the timeshare in Branson regardless of whether you own at that resort or someplace else.

## The nitty-gritty of renting timeshare

You can rent your time out to anyone else if you're not using it. Keep in mind that any time you rent out your timeshare, you have to do so through either the resort or the exchange company. In other words, just like you do when you are using it yourself, you *must* make reservations through the resort and/or the exchange company. The exception is when you're using (or renting) a fixed week at your home resort (a *fixed week* means that you don't have to make reservations, whether you use it or someone else does). Still, you should always inform the resort that someone will be using your week — you wouldn't want the resort to just give out your room to anyone claiming to be you, would you?

I highly recommend the following when renting out your timeshare:

✔ Purchase *guest certificates* from RCI and II, which work to absolve you of any liability that happens during the renters' stay; it puts the burden onto the person who is renting. These certificates range from $19 to $49, which you can and should build into the rental fee that you charge the people staying at your timeshare.

✔ Get a certified or cashier's check from your renters three weeks in advance of their check-in date. This is just a precaution, though, not a hard-and-fast rule.

✔ Advise the resort management that you won't be using the time-share, and that Joe Smith will be staying instead. This can be done via a phone call, letter, fax, or e-mail.

✔ Provide Joe Smith with a letter indicating that you, the owner, are allowing Joe Smith, the renter, to use your vacation week. Include your contact information for any questions and advise Joe to bring that letter with him on his vacation.

# How to find timeshare to rent

If you don't own timeshare, but you're curious about timeshare and interested in renting for a week rather than spending money on hotels or motels, you can rent time-shares using the following scenarios:

✔ **From the owner:** Anyone who owns timeshare can rent it to you and charge what they wish.

✔ **From the resorts:** All resorts have inventory reserved for their use as well as the use of RCI and II (the chief exchange companies; see Chapter 12). It's up to the individual resort what they do with their inventory — and many times they rent it to the public.

✔ **From marketing companies:** Some marketing companies have agreements with resorts to put their clients in timeshare units, often as a promotion to sell timeshare.

✔ **From the exchange companies:** Exchange companies sometimes rent timeshare. However, RCI (and II, to a lesser extent) is getting heat from owners because oftentimes an owner will put in a request for a trade to a specific region only to be told nothing is available or he'll have to be put on a waiting list. The owner then finds a week in that area or at that resort on a rental Web site for substantially more than the $129 or so that it would have cost to exchange into it. What owners need to know is that *exchange inventory* is different from *developer inventory* or even *RCI* (or II) *inventory*. RCI insists, however, that member weeks that are deposited for exchange are not included in any rental programs; instead, only those member weeks deposited for other services, such as cruises, are available.

As a renter, are you required to attend a timeshare presentation? Renting is just like using or exchanging. With the exception of the third bullet (when a marketing company offers promotional vacations to sell timeshare), none of the above scenarios requires that you attend a timeshare presentation. But be assured that once you're on-site, you'll almost always receive an offer — often linked to cash, meals, or other perks — to attend a *preview, resort update,* or whatever they decide to call the standard timeshare sales presentation. Know, however, that it is *not* a requirement.

# Selling Your Timeshare

Renting your week or weeks is a fine alternative if you find yourself with more timeshare than you can use in any given year. But what if you feel that the timeshare has become unnecessary, for whatever reason?

As was the case with renting, it is important to remember a few questions that you should have asked before you buy timeshare:

- Can I sell this timeshare at any time to anyone?

- Will the resort buy back my timeshare if I don't want it any longer? If so, for how much?

- If I sell to a private party, what paperwork do I need and what paperwork do they need? Do I have to pay a fee to sell my timeshare?

- If I sell to someone else, does that person own exactly what I own, with all rights and privileges?

You should never buy a timeshare with the express understanding, or even hope, of making money. Timesharing is merely an alternative to spending rental money. Timeshares can and do increase in value, however, but inflation may negate any gains you make.

## Determining the types of ownership

It is important to know what type of ownership the timeshare is in order to know who controls it legally. When you buy deeded timeshare, the developer should ask you "What type of ownership would you like this to be deeded in?"

When you purchase your timeshare originally, don't assume that the developer or whomever you are purchasing your timeshare from knows the type of ownership you want or need. It is up to you, the purchaser, to ensure you get the kind of ownership you want.

Timeshare is generally conveyed as four basic types of ownership:

- **Sole owner:** As a *sole owner,* one person enjoys title in his or her name only.

- **Joint tenancy:** *Joint tenancy* is a way of owning property, whether real estate or personal property, in the name of two or more people. The most common form of joint tenancy is *joint tenancy with right of survivorship* — when one person dies, the survivor(s) becomes the sole owner.

- **Tenancy in common:** Similar to joint tenancy, with *tenancy in common,* several owners each hold an undivided portion of the property. Each owner may deal with his or her portion of the property as she wishes (giving it away, mortgaging it, bequeathing it), and, upon death, the share becomes part of his or her estate.

✔ **Tenancy in the entirety:** *Tenancy in the entirety* is the same as joint tenancy, but solely between a husband and wife.

When you sell your timeshare (or when you purchase timeshare on the secondary market), it is vital to have the correct signatures:

✔ If the timeshare is held in sole ownership, obviously you signature alone is all that's needed to convey the title.

✔ If the timeshare is held in joint tenancy, each tenant's signature is needed. If only one person conveys his or her interest, the joint tenancy will be broken and, by default, a tenant-in-common situation is created.

✔ If the timeshare is held by tenants in common, again each tenant's signature is necessary. However, if one party signs its interest to someone else, the new owner(s) as well as the remaining owners still own an undivided interest together.

✔ If the timeshare is held by tenants in the entirety, both the husband and wife's signature are needed to convey title to another person(s).

## The nitty-gritty of selling timeshare

How do you sell timeshare? Much like you buy timeshare on the resale market (discussed in Chapter 9). Several publications, notably *TimeSharing Today* (www.tstoday.com) have an extensive listing of timeshare for sale.

In addition, many realty companies maintain a completely separate division for timeshare sales. Most, if not all, of these companies charge a fee for selling timeshare — and the fee can be quite high. Sometimes, the resort you bought your unit from will offer to buy back your timeshare. However, I have never heard of a timeshare resort that buys back its property before the resort is sold out, when it stands to make a nice profit on reselling your unit.

My advice? Advertise the timeshare yourself. This is easy to do, but it's also where the frustration sets in. Most people incorrectly assume that if they purchased a timeshare for $13,500 three years ago, they'll be able to sell it for $15,000 today. Nine times out of ten that won't be the case. You should never buy timeshare as a real estate investment or as a get-rich-quick scheme.

Hundreds of companies offering to "Buy back your timeshare!" advertise on TV and on the Internet. Some of these companies are more legitimate than others, but most charge a hefty upfront *listing fee*. Many of these companies tell you that they need your week of timeshare in order to show it properly to clients. Don't fall for this scam. These companies have no interest in selling your timeshare for you. Rather, they take your week, rent it out to someone for perhaps $1,000 or more, and leave you with nothing. You can easily do this yourself; and, as discussed in the

"Renting Your Timeshare" section, most people make their money back quicker and with less aggravation by renting out their timeshare for a number of years, not by selling it.

# Willing Your Timeshare

What happens to your timeshare property when you or the co-owner dies and the timeshare is to be willed?

First of all, it's important to know the type of ownership your timeshare is, and whether or not it can be willed (see "Determining the types of ownership" section).

When the timeshare is deeded in perpetuity, it generally means that it can be willed or passed on to the heirs. There are, however, exceptions (that is, certain timeshare resorts *make* exceptions), so always check the fine print before you buy anything.

Timeshares that are deeded right-to-use can also be willed, although there is often a time or usage limit attached (see Chapter 3).

 Some timeshare resorts don't allow the property to be willed and, therefore, allow only the purchaser to use the timeshare and the associated benefits. If being able to will your timeshare is important to you, stay away from these resorts — plenty of timeshare resorts do allow you to will the property and/or usage.

Just as the different types of ownership impact how a timeshare is sold, they also impact what happens in the case of death:

✔ In the event of your death as a sole owner, the title will pass on to your heirs or your estate either by your will or through the laws of intestacy (that is, if you don't have a valid will).

✔ In the event of your death if you're one of the joint tenants, your interest will pass to the surviving joint tenant.

✔ In the case of your death as one of the tenants in common, the title will pass on to your heirs either by will or laws of intestacy.

✔ In the case of your death as one of the tenants by the entirety (that is, if you hold the property with your spouse), your spouse will have complete title.

 The material covered in this book, including this chapter, is not intended, nor should be construed, as the law in every case. I am merely providing a framework. Consult your lawyer or attorney for specific questions regarding willing or trusting timeshare or any other property or asset.

# Chapter 16

# Looking Beyond Traditional Timeshare

*In This Chapter*

▶ Signing up for vacation clubs

▶ Doing the town with urban timeshare

▶ Talking about fractionals, hotel condos, and private residence clubs

*T*imeshare has branched out into many different incarnations, from high-end fractionals and private residence clubs to vacation clubs to urban interval ownerships. This chapter gives you a look at each.

## Buying into Vacation Clubs

Vacation clubs have been around almost as long as timeshare. For many people, these clubs offer an alternative to hotel accommodations without the commitment, either financially or mentally, that a timeshare generally demands. And that's usually the selling point that vacation clubs pitch to potential customers. It goes something like: "We know what you like about timeshare — the choice of high-quality resorts — and we know what you don't like about timeshare — the large upfront costs, the annual maintenance fees, and the long-term commitment. So what if you could get all the benefits without any of the drawbacks?"

### The nitty-gritty of vacation clubs

Although the details may differ from one vacation club to another, here is the basic premise: For a one-time enrollment or membership fee, members have the opportunity to stay at a timeshare resort one or more times a year for a fee that's less than they would expect to pay if they were coming in off the street. In addition, members generally have access to a travel company or travel agency that may offer discounts on hotel stays, cruises, airfare, package tour vacations, and the like.

Vacation clubs often offer tremendous deals on nontimeshare vacations. In November and December 2004, for example, one club was offering a five-day, four-night package to Amsterdam including round-trip airfare from New York, breakfast everyday, and a sightseeing tour of Amsterdam — for $399. In some cases, vacation clubs offer the most value if you don't use timeshare weeks at all, and you're under no obligation to ever use any weeks of timeshare.

All benefits of a vacation club may be used by members' families as well as willed.

Here is an actual example of three different packages offered by a vacation club headquartered in Florida:

✔ Package #1:

- Enrollment fee of $4,995

- Access to four weeks of timeshare annually

- Discounts on other vacation components

✔ Package #2:

- Enrollment fee of $3,995

- Access to two weeks of timeshare annually

- Discounts on other vacation components

✔ Package #3:

- Enrollment fee of $2,995

- Access to one week of timeshare annually

- Discounts on other vacation components

✔ Annual dues: $149

✔ Average cost of timeshare weeks: $500

## Assessing the value of vacation clubs

Is a vacation club the way to go? Take a look at some numbers, based on a $100 hotel room with 8% tax and 10% annual inflation on rooms and timeshare weeks.

|  | Hotel/Taxes | Vacation Club/2 Weeks |
| --- | --- | --- |
| Year 1 | $1,400/$112 | $3,995/$1,000 |
| Year 2 | $1,540/$123 | 0/$1,100 |
| Year 3 | $1,694/$135 | 0/$1,210 |
| Year 4 | $1,863/$149 | 0/$1,331 |
| Year 5 | $2,049/$163 | 0/$1,464 |
| Year 6 | $2,253/$180 | 0/$1,610 |

| Year 7 | $2,478/$198 | 0/$1,771 |
| Year 8 | $2,725/$218 | 0/$1,948 |
| Year 9 | $2,997/$239 | 0/$2,143 |
| Year 10 | $3,296/$263 | 0/$2,357 |
| Total spent | $22,295/$1,780 | $3,995/$15,934 |
| Grand Total | $24,075 | $19,929 |

This isn't a huge savings by any standard, and don't forget, for your $19,929 expenditure, you own *nothing*. In a reversal of the guiding economic principles of timeshare, in this case, if you use your vacation club lodging only for a few years, rather than for ten years, you realize more savings.

Where do these vacation clubs get their timeshare weeks? In many instances, they're getting *RCI Bonus weeks* and/or *II Getaway weeks*. These weeks from the leading exchange companies (see Chapter 12) are generally excess weeks of timeshare that the exchange companies cannot fill with actual members. Using these weeks, your chances are almost nil of getting a good week in a good location.

However, some vacation clubs go a step further and actually have agreements with resort developers to gain access to inventory that's not even available to the RCI or II pool. Needless to say, these particular vacation clubs have better inventory, and your chances of getting a good week in a good location increase substantially.

## Asking the right questions

As with exchanging your timeshare for a week at another resort, it is absolutely not necessary to go through a timeshare presentation if you don't want to. Understand that someone from the resort will contact you, possibly several times during your stay, and offer you gifts of various values, but you are *not* obligated to attend a timeshare presentation when using timeshare weeks through a vacation club.

Just as you have a list of questions to ask when purchasing a timeshare, here are some questions to pose when buying into a vacation club:

- ✔ Is this product willable and/or transferable?
- ✔ Where does the vacation club obtain its timeshare weeks from?
- ✔ What happens if the vacation club goes out of business?
- ✔ Is the vacation club a member of the Better Business Bureau?

Unfortunately, there are many examples of vacation clubs that promised the moon and delivered nothing. Do your due diligence with any vacation club — because you're not purchasing a deed, you have fewer legal rights than you would with a timeshare.

# Discovering Urban Timeshare

Not so long ago the word "timeshare" conjured up beachfront properties, high-rise towers near mega attractions, or condos perched near ski slopes.

But now when you hear the word timeshare, you're just as likely to imagine the wharves of London, the hills of San Francisco, the shopping streets of Paris, and even all that midtown Manhattan has to offer. Welcome to the wonderful world of urban timeshares!

If you would rather attend the opera than recline on a beach chair, listen to the symphony than brave long lines at a theme park, shop at upscale boutiques than buy a T-shirt at a theme-park emporium, or take in the sights from the top of the Empire State Building than dig for clams, a timeshare in the middle of a bustling city is just the tonic.

Just like its noncity counterparts, urban timeshare offers more than a typical hotel room; most have a kitchenette, separate living and sleeping areas, and the most notable feature: more space than the average hotel room. At the Manhattan Club, for example, suites sleep four people and average about 650 square feet — nearly twice the space of an average hotel room in New York City.

What the urban timeshares lack in terms of access to recreational activities, outdoor sports facilities, and beaches or ski lifts, they make up for in terms of prime city locations. New York City's Manhattan Club is just across the street from Carnegie Hall and only three blocks from Central Park. San Francisco's Club Donatello is only one block from Union Square. The Grand Residence is located in Mayfair, one of the most prestigious (and costly) districts in London.

I had always suspected that most of the timeshares at the Manhattan Club in New York City were owned by companies who used them for business purposes. I was happily surprised, however, to find out that individuals and families comprise the majority of the ownership, proving that savvy consumers are taking advantage of the myriad vacation options not only in timeshare but in the entire hospitality industry.

If you plan to drive to your urban timeshare, always ask whether parking is included in the purchase price. While you wouldn't think of asking whether you could park your car for free at a timeshare resort in Myrtle Beach, South Carolina, or Branson, Missouri, it's a different story in cities like New York City, Boston, and Paris. These are walking cities, where cars are more of a hindrance than a help, and if you drive, you want to find long-term parking for your car during the duration of your stay.

Although urban timeshares are often more costly than their beach, mountain, or wilderness counterparts, they do enjoy very high trading power. Why? The supply is low. If New York City has only one timeshare resort with less than 400 rooms, it doesn't take a lot of requests to overrun supply. Remember that both RCI and II take into account supply as well as demand when fulfilling trades.

# Snapshot: Las Vegas timeshare

Vegas has been a boomtown for more than 50 years and shows no sign of slowing down. Nothing is understated or done on a small scale here.

Just as hotels keep being torn down and rebuilt bigger and brassier than before, the timeshare market is growing at an equally rapid rate. Plans are in the works to build at least seven or eight large-scale (more than 1,000 rooms each) timeshare resorts on or right off the strip.

II lists 12 resorts in their latest directory, five of them right on the famed Las Vegas Strip, (otherwise known as Las Vegas Blvd. South). RCI lists 13 properties, with five right on the strip and three on properties that have casinos.

It stands to reason that if timeshares in Las Vegas are being built at a rapid rate, what passes for timeshare marketing is also growing. However, some of the worst marketing practices are found here.

OPCs, or off-property consultants, are rife throughout the city. Everywhere you go, you see offers for "FREE DINNER SHOW TICKETS," "DISCOUNTED SHOW TICKETS," "$50 GAMING CREDITS," and other come-ons to lure you into a timeshare presentation. One well-known independent company hires women in low-cut, tight-fitting T-shirts and Spandex pants to lure clients in. Once inside the timeshare resort, clients are subjected to high-pressure sales tactics.

More so than in almost any other timeshare location, it's important to maintain a clear head when contemplating timeshare in Las Vegas. Don't be blinded by the flashing lights and the glitz of the place. Everything in Las Vegas has flashing lights and a high glitz factor — it's often there to hide what's really going on.

That said, Las Vegas has some very fine and reputable timeshare companies doing good business without resorting to tired, worn-out timeshare tricks.

A few pointers to keep in mind:

✔ Las Vegas, like Orlando, is "all red (peak season), all the time" and will generally get you a decent exchange.

✔ Ask yourself whether you plan to spend a full week in Las Vegas when you visit. If not, don't exchange into Vegas and give up an entire week.

✔ Because of the short lifetime of many hotels and timeshare properties in Las Vegas, you have to ask some very pertinent questions about what happens to your deed, your property, your rights, and the like should the resort be sold, torn down, or put under new management.

✔ If you plan a trip to Las Vegas either as your home resort or on a trade, be sure to find out when the big conventions are in town — and try to avoid being there during those times. Although you'll never see Las Vegas empty — and that's part of its lure, right? — trying to navigate the Strip during one of the world's largest computer conferences is something you want to avoid.

## Exploring Fractionals and Private Residence Clubs

Fractionals are the fastest-growing segment of the timeshare industry, and without a doubt the most costly. With *fractionals,* the purchaser owns a multiple number of weeks (typically a fraction of a year: one-quarter, one-eighteenth, or one-thirteenth). Timeshares that operate as fractionals are typically run by management companies and have sizeable annual maintenance fees as well as membership fees.

With prices starting at $100,000 to upwards of $500,000, fractionals can't be considered traditional timesharing in any sense of the word. Fractionals are financially out of reach for families who generally spend less than $2,000 per year on vacation. For those consumers who demand the best, want something out of the ordinary, and have the money, fractionals represent the wave of the future in vacationing.

Close cousins of the fractional, condominium hotels, hotel residences (see the "Discovering Urban Timeshare" section), and private residence clubs (PRCs) are making a huge impact in both the vacation and real estate arenas. *Private residence clubs* are ultraluxurious properties found in the most desired locations around the world. They come complete with automobiles, private chefs, and full-time personal assistants and offer many of the same amenities as country clubs.

Condominium hotels are becoming a popular alternative to the traditional vacation or second home. It's simple, really: You purchase a luxury hotel unit for a set price, pay a monthly maintenance fee to maintain the room and the grounds, and use it when you want to with no need for reservations. Hotel residences and private residence clubs, such as the Trump International Hotel and Tower scheduled to open in Chicago in 2007 and the Mandarin Oriental in New York, are examples of timesharing that really isn't timesharing at all, but more like primary (well, make that secondary) residences.

Condo hotels, hotel residences, and private residence clubs can be considered more of a real estate investment than a traditional timeshare. One of the caveats of traditional timeshare for the buyer to realize is that timeshare should never be purchased as a real estate or even a rental investment.

While fractionals do allow owners to trade or exchange within a network, most owners buy at a location that they enjoy returning to year after year, unlike traditional timeshare, in which exchanging is one of the most popular features and among the key reasons consumers purchase.

## The nitty-gritty of fractionals

What is fractional? Fractionals differ from timeshare in these four key ways:

- ✔ You own more than a week or two of vacation time a year. In a fractional timeshare, you own anywhere from one month to four months of the year. You generally purchase the time (or shares) from the management company, and that company handles the maintenance fees as well as scheduling time.

- ✔ Fractionals offer substantially higher quality amenities than even the best traditional timeshare can offer.

- ✔ Fractionals have substantially higher prices ($100,000 and up) as well as higher maintenance fees.

- ✔ Fractionals have substantially greater satisfaction rates (traditional timeshare registers at a 85% to 88% satisfaction rate, while fractionals register at a 96% satisfaction rate).

As with timeshares, fractionals may or may not be deeded real estate. Always ask. Just as you must ask some basic questions when considering a timeshare for $13,500, you should ask even more questions before plopping $150,000 on the table.

Some fractionals are more like timeshare condos, albeit with more amenities; others may be suites in a high-end, luxury hotel, generally found in urban areas.

As of March 2004, there were 151 resorts that offered fractional ownership worldwide, with the vast majority (132) in the United States. Note that these numbers do not include single homes sold on a fractional basis, nor properties with a small number of condominiums that are made available on a fractional basis.

Almost 50% of the fractional resorts are located in ski areas, while beach areas account for about 30% of the market. The remaining 20% is split between golf and urban locations.

|  | *Average Prices* | *Price Per Week* |
| --- | --- | --- |
| Traditional | $123,100 | $12,310 |
| High end | $165,800 | $33,160 |
| Private residence | $247,000 | $49,400 |

Table 16-1 shows you the differences between traditional timeshare and fractionals.

**Table 16-1     Traditional Timeshare versus Fractionals**

|  | *Timeshare* | *Fractional* |
| --- | --- | --- |
| **Cost** | Average of $13,500 from developer, often considerably less on resale market. Average yearly maintenance fee of about $500. | Generally start at $100,000, some with yearly fees over $10,000. |
| **Exclusivity** | Not very exclusive; marketed and sometimes sold to just about anyone, especially if purchased on the resale market. Look at it this way: You and roughly 51 other people own the same condo. | Very exclusive, in large part due to the high cost. These are not marketed to just anyone and have an exclusive country-club feel. At most, you and 11 other people own the same condo/home. |
| **Type of residence** | Generally more luxurious than a traditional hotel/motel room, offering kitchens, living rooms, larger bathrooms, and so on. | Far more luxurious than even a traditional time-share, most fractionals look and feel more like a private house than an enhanced hotel room. |
| **Length of ownership per year** | Purchased by the week, with the average owner owning one or two weeks per year. | Most fractionals start at one-twelfth of the year (four weeks) and many go to one-quarter of the year (three months) or more. |
| **Locations** | More than 5,700 time-shares around the world. | Limited areas, which adds to the exclusivity factor. |
| **Financing options** | Banks will not finance timeshares with a traditional mortgage, so often consumers use the developers' extraordinarily high financing rate: on average 15.9%. | More and more banks are treating fractionals as a conventional second home. |

| | Timeshare | Fractional |
|---|---|---|
| **Real estate appreciation possibilities** | Although some timeshares have gone up in value, the general rule is that if you can sell it ten years down the road for what you paid for it, you've done extraordinarily well. Don't buy a timeshare as a real estate investment; it simply isn't. | Significantly better than a traditional timeshare, but still less than a single-family house. |
| **Services available** | Limited to sports facilities, a few restaurants on-site, transportation to area attractions and shopping. | The sky is the limit: private dinner parties, butler service, personal shopping, arranging to have your skis waxed and ready for your arrival, use of private jet. |
| **Trading** | Most people purchase a timeshare for the exchanging possibilities, with various degrees of success depending on where they own. Even notoriously poor locations for trading can generally be exchanged for something, provided you aren't that picky about where you end up, due to the sheer number of timeshare locations available. | Most people purchase a fractional for the location and resort quality. Some exchanging does occur, but because of the very low number of fractional products available, the tendency is to purchase where you want to vacation. A typical fractional owner is simply not going to want to trade one of his or her $20,000+ weeks for a week in a traditional timeshare on a crowded beach next to everyone and their mothers-in-law. |

## What to expect of a fractional

What kind of services and amenities can you expect with fractionals? Although the list varies from property to property, the following gives you a good idea of the type of high-end features available. Of course, most of these extra services come with extra fees.

> ✔ Airport pickup
>
> ✔ Groceries and toiletries supplied before arrival
>
> ✔ Clothing (sent ahead) unpacked and put away before arrival
>
> ✔ Arrangement of complete leisure or business itinerary, complete with luxury car rental or chauffeured limousine
>
> ✔ 24-hour room service
>
> ✔ Daily housekeeping including laundry
>
> ✔ Butler service
>
> ✔ Private chefs and personalized menus
>
> ✔ Childcare

Fractional timeshares are for the most part more cost advantageous for the developer than traditional timeshare, so it was only a matter of time before other luxury products and services were thrown into the fray. Some of the latest perks include

> ✔ Jets and other planes
>
> ✔ Recreational vehicles
>
> ✔ Yachts and other boats

When you aren't using your fractional, you can generally rent it out yourself, or for a fee, the management company will rent it for you. But renting your hotel property when you aren't using it may not be cost effective — some management fees are as much as 50%.

Purchasing one of these properties should be handled with the same degree of preparation, use of professionals (lawyers, real estate agents, and so on), and care that you handle your primary residence with.

# Part V
# The Part of Tens

The 5th Wave                    By Rich Tennant

"Maybe we shouldn't have gotten a timeshare so close to the Everglades."

## *In this part . . .*

I list several timeshare sales pitches you should run, not walk, away from and show you how timeshare has branched out to become much more than just a condominium unit. I also tell you ten things to keep in mind before buying timeshare.

# Chapter 17

# Ten Timeshare Sales Situations You Should Run, Not Walk, Away From

. . . . . . . . . . . . . . . . . . . . . . . . . . . . . . . . . . . . . . . . . . . . . . . .

### In This Chapter

▶ Picking up on sleazy timeshare sales tactics

▶ Finding out there's no free lunch

▶ Dealing with aggressive timeshare salespersons

. . . . . . . . . . . . . . . . . . . . . . . . . . . . . . . . . . . . . . . . . . . . . . . .

*T*he sleazy days of timeshare fraud are largely fading from view, although you can be sure that wherever money is involved, scam artists will find creative ways to take yours. It's sad but true: Year after year, some timeshare salespersons continue to pitch heat. Here are ten . . . er, make that twelve . . . timeshare sales pitches and situations that should have you heading for the door, checkbook firmly tucked away.

## Free Vacation! Er . . . Uh, Except For . . .

The fine print for your free timeshare vacation states that the receipt of one portion of the offer (the airline ticket) is dependent on the purchase of something else (hotel accommodations).

## You Can't Afford Not to Buy It!

High-pressure sales presentations often reach this arm-twisting conclusion at some point in the pitch — or some variation of it, such as "Only a fool would walk away from this deal!" or "You have to do this now!" Then there's "You owe it to your children" — a bottom-of-the-barrel ploy that is aimed directly at the heartstrings. A variation on the latter is "You owe it" to a long-suffering spouse, for whom a life reward is evidently due.

## Shaquille O'Neal Practices on Our Basketball Court!

Oh and he's even looking to start a pickup game with the local timeshare owners. If you think that Shaquille O'Neal

- ✔ Doesn't own his own basketball court
- ✔ Needs to use the half-court at a timeshare to hone his game

have I got a bridge in Brooklyn for you!

## They Do Look Awfully Familiar

The happy couple enjoying an exotic vacation in the sales brochure bears a distinct resemblance to the timeshare salesperson and his assistant.

## Give Us Money So We Can Give You More Money

You may receive a postcard or fax of promotional mailings that require you to pay a fee or to purchase membership in a travel club in order to claim a vacation or travel prize.

 If someone asks you for money in advance to pay for a special vacation — whether by phone, fax, or snail mail — don't do it. And don't under any circumstances give your credit card number out to anyone offering a free vacation.

## After You Pay Off Your Timeshare, You Vacation for Free

This is simply not true. You have to pay maintenance fees and/or taxes, exchange fees, special assessments, and of course transportation, food, shopping, and the like. Vacations are never free.

## For You, We Cut the Price in Half!

You are special, it's true, but if you hear these words: "Normally we charge $28,000 for a two-bedroom timeshare, but because you're here with us today, you can have the exact same thing for only $14,000," head for the door. Car dealers are infamous for the same silly pitch. Do you really think that a timeshare developer is going to give you a $14,000 discount simply because they like you? Always ask upfront whether you'll be given more than one price. And know that in 2004, the average price of a two-bedroom timeshare in the United States was $13,500.

## Your Timeshare Hasn't Been Built Yet

You're shown a beachfront timeshare unit that's spacious, good-quality, and just right for you. You get back to the sales tent, ready to buy. "By the way," the salesperson says, "the timeshare we showed you is not the one for sale — your timeshare hasn't been built yet." See ya.

## Free Tequila!

When a timeshare salesperson reaches for the alcohol, it's time to take cover. This is a fairly common sales ploy among unsavory timeshare operators in places like Mexico and the Caribbean, where a few glasses of tequila work to loosen your inhibitions — and your purse strings.

## Versailles Is on the Brochure Cover

No kidding: I once saw a timeshare company brochure that showed King Ludwig's 19th-century fairy-tale palace, Neuschwanstein, in Bavaria on the cover as a timeshare property. Now that's taking bait-and-switch to another level.

## You'll Make It All Back in Rentals

You're at a timeshare presentation in Cancun and the salesperson tells you that the timeshare you are about to purchase will rent for lots of money and that you can count on this money to pay for the down payment or the full purchase of the timeshare membership. I first heard about this one in the helpful Web site *The Timeshare Beat* (www.thetimeshare beat.com). Salespeople even go so far as to have the resort "owner" talk to you on the phone while you're still in the sales room in Mexico or fax you a document guaranteeing that rental. As the good people at *The Timeshare Beat* advise: Beware of any promises made to you about rental or resale value.

## You're Wasting My Time Here!

Timeshare presentations can stretch into hours of high-pressure tactics, with salespersons handing off potential customers to sales staff who ratchet up the hard sell. One final tactic — that, sadly, works in some situations — is when a salesperson pretends to get angry and even insults the buyer by questioning his or her intelligence for balking at the deal. Fortunately, this tactic is generally used by second- and third-rate companies only; the established brands rarely apply this sort of hard-sell to selling timeshare anymore.

# Chapter 18

# Ten Timeshares You May Not Have Thought of As Timeshare

*In This Chapter*
▶ Discovering a world of timeshare destinations
▶ Exploring the many types of timeshare

*M*any people who hear the word "timeshare" envision a monotonous series of concrete condos shadowing a beach. But the staying power of timeshare is a direct result of the industry's efforts to stay fresh and competitive and give consumers more, better choices. Sure, dull cookie-cutter timeshares are still around, but so is a growing variety of novel timeshares around the world. Open an RCI or II directory (those are the leading timeshare exchange companies — see Chapter 12) to virtually any page, and you can see how varied the options are. Here are ten — well, really fifteen, but who's counting? — timeshare offerings you may never have thought of as timeshare.

## Canal Boats in England

Cruise through the English countryside in a fully equipped canal boat.

## Sailboats in St. Vincent

Spend your timeshare week of sailing and swimming in the Caribbean on your own private boat.

## Forest Chalets in Georgia

Three-bedroom chalets are available in the forested mountains of Georgia.

## Cabins in New Mexico

Fully equipped cabins with decks are within view of hot-air balloonists.

## Rooms in a 17th-Century French Castle

Stay in a towered and turreted castle in the Loire Valley with panoramic views of the French countryside.

## Private Cruising in Antigua

Spend a week sailing your own yacht, stopping for picnics and swims on the island's hundreds of private beaches.

## Thatch-Roofed Cottages in Belize

These jungle homes let you watch monkeys swinging just outside your bedroom window.

## Villas in The Gambia

Stay in cottage villas on stilts within view of African wildlife reserves.

## Terraced Apartments in South Africa

Apartments with sea views are available in both Cape Town and Durban.

## Country Lodges in New Zealand

Spend a week in a rustic New Zealand lodge with two swimming pools, a spa, and a gourmet restaurant.

## Golf Resorts in China

Enjoy a suite overlooking uniquely landscaped Chinese courses.

## Ski Parks in Switzerland

Learn to ski some of the finest mountains in the world, and have your après-ski at home in your timeshare, in front of your own fireplace.

## Beach Clubs in Hawaii

Stay in a beachfront bungalow set inside a multi-million-dollar club.

## Garden Villas in Italy

Spend your timeshare week in a historic garden villa just minutes by water taxi from St. Mark's Square.

## Country Clubs in England

Enjoy tea with other guests in the main room of a Tudor manse.

# Chapter 19

# Ten Things About Timeshare Every Consumer Should Know

*In This Chapter*
▶ Getting savvy about timeshare
▶ Knowing when to buy and when not to buy

*T*imeshare is a commodity and a business, and anyone thinking of buying timeshare should do his or her best to become a thoroughly informed consumer before signing anything. Here are ten issues you should know about buying timeshare.

## Understand Why the Price Is What It Is

The average cost of a two-bedroom timeshare in 2004 was $13,500. Anything substantially higher or lower than that, and you should be asking, "Why?"

## Define "Best" for Yourself

There is no such thing as the "best" timeshare. It's imperative to purchase the timeshare that will allow you to use it for what you need. For some people, Orlando is best; for others, Orlando would be a waste of money.

# Timeshare Isn't a Real Estate Investment

Never buy timeshare as a real estate investment. It isn't. Look at the long-term picture. Sure, for many people, $13,500 is a lot of money, but if you're shelling out $100 for hotel rooms ten nights a year anyway, it would take only 13 years to break even versus hotel costs. And that's before you factor in the inevitable hotel inflation. And anything after 13 years is gravy.

# Get the Lowdown on Maintenance Fees

Ask about the maintenance fees. More than likely, you will be charged annual maintenance fees. Questions to ask include

- ✔ How much are they?
- ✔ How much did they go up from last year to this year?
- ✔ Who controls them? (In other words, are owners included on the resort's controlling board?)

# Remember What Happens When You Assume

Assume nothing. A lot of timeshare are deeded in perpetuity. Many are not. Most timeshare operates on a points-based system (see Chapter 7). Often, those points are not inflation-proof. Always ask and don't be afraid to say "no" if the product doesn't suit your needs or wants.

# Never Buy Because of Incentives

Although it may be high-pressure, low-pressure, or (I hope) no-pressure, you will be asked to buy right there on the spot, and you'll be offered incentives to do so. Never buy because of the incentives. Buy only if you answer "yes" to these three questions:

- ✔ Do you like the product and/or the particular resort?
- ✔ If you owned it, would you use it? This means that you plan or intend to spend that amount of money anyway, renting hotels/motels/condos on vacation. (Note the word "plan." To quote the advertisement, "You can't predict; you can plan.")
- ✔ Are you willing to fit the monthly payment into your budget?

## *You Can — and Should — Negotiate*

Almost everything is negotiable, if you ask. It's true. Price, interest rates (most timeshare offer in-house financing), and perks (such as first-year membership dues or first-year maintenance fees) are often negotiable.

## *You Can't Believe Everything You Hear*

Don't believe everything you hear. That goes from Uncle Paul telling you that timeshare doesn't work because he was never able to trade to go anywhere else to the salesperson telling you that you'll always be able to trade at any time for any place.

## *Free, Perfect, Always, and Never Don't Exist*

In general, stay clear of anyone, especially timeshare salespersons, that use the words *free, perfect, always,* and/or *never.* These absolutes don't exist.

## *You Don't Have to Sit through the Pitch*

You're free to ask to see any timeshare resort and get pricing information without having to sit through a monotonous, tedious, and time-consuming sales pitch.

# Appendix A

# Quick Concierge

## Exchange Companies

### Interval International (II)

World Headquarters: P.O. Box 41920
6262 Sunset Dr., Miami, FL 33243-1920

Web site: www.intervalworld.com
General information: ☎ 800-843-8843

### Deposit and/or Exchange Weeks

☎ 800-634-3415
305-666-1884
305-665-1918 (Spanish)
305-667-5321 (fax)
☎ 800-822-6522 (TDD), Mon–Fri
9 a.m.–5 p.m.

### Interval Travel Services

P.O. Box 431920
Miami, FL 33243-1920
Mon–Fri 9 a.m.–11 p.m.
Sat, Sun, and holidays:
10 a.m.–8 p.m.

**Airline, Hotel, Car Rental**
☎ 800-235-4000
305-666-4063
305-667-5272 (fax)

### Overseas Offices

#### United Kingdom

Interval International Limited
Coombe Hill House
Beverley Way
London SW20 0AR

**Vacation Packages**
☎ 800-772-1861
305-666-1884, ext. 7519

**Getaway Availability**
☎ 800-722-1860
24 hours a day

**Getaway Reservations**
☎ 800-772-1880
305-666-1884, ext. 7504
Mon–Fri 9 a.m.–11 p.m.
Sat, Sun, and holidays:
10 a.m.– 8 p.m.

**Tours/Adventure Travel**
☎ 800-949-2222
305-668-3465
305-598-4093 (fax)

**Cruises**
☎ 800-622-1540
305-668-3496
305-598-4093 (fax)

☎ 44-870-744-222
44-870-7444-217 (fax)

Languages Spoken: English, Arabic,
Dutch, French, Greek

### Singapore

Interval International Singapore
(Pte) Ltd.
One Phillip Street
#09-00
Singapore 048692

☎ 65-6318-2500
65-6318-2511 (fax)

Languages spoken: English, Bahasa
Indonesian, Cantonese, Malay,
Mandarin, Thai

### Mexico

Intercambios Internacionales de
Vacaciones S.A de C.V
Edificio Torre Caballito
Paseo de la Reforma No. 10, Piso 9
Colonia Centro, Delegación
Cuauhtémoc
06300 Mexico, D.F.

☎ 52-5-627-7300
52-5-627-7310 (fax)

Languages spoken: English, Spanish

*Note:* Additionally, Interval International member services are also available in
Argentina, Australia, Boliva, Brazil, Chile, Columbia, Costa Rica, Czech Republic,
Denmark, Egypt, Finland, France, Germany, Greece, Guatamala, Hong Kong,
Hungary, India, Indonesia, Israel, Italy, Japan, Malaysia, The Netherlands, New
Zealand, Norway, Panama, Paraguay, Peru, Philippines, Poland, Portugal, Russia,
Spain, Sweden, Taiwan, Thailand, Turkey, Uruguay, and Venezuela.

## Resort Condominiums International (RCI)

**Member Services** (reservations,
information, points partners program
or cruises)

☎ 877-969-7476
317-805-9335 (fax)

Mon–Fri 8 a.m. to midnight, Sat
9 a.m.–5:30 p.m., Sun 10 a.m.–6:30 p.m.

Memorial Day, Independence Day,
Labor Day, Christmas Eve, and
New Year's Day: 9 a.m.–6 p.m.
Closed: Easter, Thanksgiving Day,
and Christmas Day

Web site: www.rci.com

## RCI Points

P.O. Box 80600
Indianapolis, IN 46280

## RCI Travel

☎ 800-654-5817

Mon–Fri 7 a.m.–7 p.m., Sat 7 a.m.–
3:30 p.m.

## Platinum Interchange

1300 North Kellogg Dr., Suite B
Anaheim, CA 92807

☎ 800-854-2324 or 714-779-7900
714-970-0273 (fax)

Web site: www.platinum
interchange.com

fun@platinuminterchange.com

## Trading Places International

23807 Aliso Creek Rd.
Laguna Niguel, CA 92656

☎ 800-365-1048 or 949-448-5150
949-448-5140 (fax)

Web site: www.tradingplaces.com
E-mail: info@tradingplaces.com

## Hawaii Timeshare Exchange

P.O. Box 1077
Koloa, HI 96756

☎ 866-860-4873 or 808-240-5316
808-742-0128 (fax)

Web site: www.htse.net
E-mail: skunz@htse.net

## Donita's Dial an Exchange

2845 Nimitz Blvd., Suite E
San Diego, CA 92106

☎ 800-468-1799 or 619-226-2776
619-226-2555 (fax)

Web site: www.dialanexchange.us
E-mail: info@dialanexchange.us

## San Francisco Exchange

185 Berry St., Suite 5411
San Francisco, CA 94107

☎ 800-739-9969 or 415-979-0870
415-979-0880 (fax)

Web site: www.sfx-resorts.com
E-mail: vacations@sfx-resorts.com

## American Resort Development Association (ARDA)

1201 15th St. N.W., Suite 400
Washington, D.C. 20005

☎ 202-371-6700
202-289-8544 (fax)

Web site: www.arda.org

## Marriott Vacation Club International

6649 Westwood Blvd., Suite 500
Orlando, FL 32821-6090

☎ 407-206-6000
407-513-6941 (fax)

Web site: www.vacationclub.com

## Hyatt Vacation Club

450 Carillon Parkway
Suite 210
St. Petersburg, FL 33716

☎ 727-803-9400

Web site: www.hyattvacationclub.com

## Starwood Vacation Ownership, Inc.

9002 San Marco Court
Orlando, FL 32819

☎ 800-869-1166, ext. 6828

Web site: www.starwoodvo.com

## Fairfield

☎ 800-786-4476

Web site: www.fairfield
resorts.com

## Disney Vacation Club

☎ 800-500-3990

Web site: www.disneyvacation
club.com

## Shell Vacations LLC/Shell Vacations Club

40 Skokie Blvd.
Suite 350
Northbrook, IL 60062

☎ 847-564-4600

Web site: www.shellvacations
club.com

# Legal Issues/Complaints

For information on timeshare issues that have been or are being addressed by the Federal Trade Commission in the USA, go to www.ftc.gov/search. Type the word **timeshare** in the search box. (*Note:* The information that will be retrieved goes back to the mid 1980s.)

You may file a complaint with the FTC by going to www.ftc.gov.

If you have a complaint about a company that offers to resell timeshares, write to:

> Correspondence Branch
> Federal Trade Commission
> Washington, D.C. 20580

> Although the FTC cannot intervene in individual disputes, the information you provide may indicate a pattern of possible law violations requiring action by the commission.

# Appendix B

# Timeshare Glossary

· · · · · · · · · · · · · · · · · · · · · · · · · · · · · · · · · · · · · · · · · · ·

Timeshare, like any other industry, has developed its own lingo. In this appendix, I define the terms that you need to know.

**alternate year (EOY):** A purchase or membership option whereby the owner or member has use of the purchase every other year. Typically, these products are at a lower cost and are used as an entry level or starter program. They may be upgraded to an annual product if the seller allows. Always inquire what the fee is to upgrade.

**American Resort Development Association (ARDA):** The professional regulator association for the timeshare industry.

**down payment:** The amount of money that the owner is required to tender to purchase the product. Typically, down payments range from 10% to 20% of the purchase price. Be sure to ask if the entire down payment is refunded, should you cancel the contract. *See also* **recession period.**

**deed:** A legal document providing title to your property, giving you ownership rights.

**deeded property:** Deeded property in timeshare is similar in many ways to deeded property in anything else: It gives the buyer ownership rights of the property. Most deeded timeshare is deeded in perpetuity, but some is deeded for 99 years due to such legal issues as land restrictions. *See also* **nondeeded property.**

**exchange:** The ability of the owner or member to use his or her product at another place and/or at another time. Typically, there is a fee assessed each time an exchange takes place. *See also* **exchange fee.**

**exchange company:** The company that does the exchanging or trading of timeshare. Generally this company is RCI (Resort Condominiums International) or II (Interval International). Ask whether there is a membership fee and whether you (or the resort) are responsible for the fee.

**exchange fee:** The fee that an exchange company charges the owner to exchange or trade a week/unit for another week/unit at another time and/or place.

**financing terms:** The terms of the loan and the annual percentage of interest that the seller offers you in order to purchase the product. Typically, timeshare is offered at extraordinarily high interest rates (roughly 16%). Be sure to ask what your options are in lowering these high interest rates.

**fixed week:** A type of ownership in which the owner has access to a specific week of the year.

**floating week:** A type of ownership in which the owner has access to a week of the year, but needs to reserve a specific week each year.

**fractional:** A type of ownership in which the owner has access to more than one or two weeks a year. Typically, fractionals are periods of four weeks to four months.

**Homeowners' association (HOA):** The membership of a resort's homeowners' association is comprised of the timeshare owners, who elect a board to administer rules and regulations.

**Interval International (II):** One of the two major timeshare exchange companies. *See also* **Resort Condominiums International (RCI).**

**leasehold:** A contract in which all or a portion of the real estate is subject to the lease, the expiration or end of which will terminate the use. This is not the same as a deed, which is in effect until sold.

**maintenance fees:** The amount of money that the owner is charged every year to maintain the property. Be certain to ask what is covered in the maintenance fees, how often the fees have gone up in the past five years, whether there is a legal cap to how much they can be raised, and whether you have a vote in the issuance of these fees. Note that if your maintenance fees (and taxes) are not current, you will not be able to use your timeshare either at the place of purchase or to exchange.

**monthly payment:** The amount of money that the owner is required to tender each month to the seller to use the product. Many resorts offer you a choice of a coupon book or an automatic debit. If you choose a coupon book, there is likely to be an additional bank fee. On a humorous note, many salespeople and sales managers prefer to use the term *monthly investment* or *monthly savings.* Don't be misled — it's a monthly payment.

**nondeeded property:** This is timeshare property that's yours to own for a set number of years or set number of uses. *See also* **deeded property.**

**points:** A type of ownership or membership in which the owner purchases an allotment of points that can be spent to obtain lodging or other benefits such as airline tickets, car rentals, and so on.

**real estate license:** The legal license issued to the person selling you timeshare. In the case of deeded property, most states require the seller to have this legal license, although some do not. It's a good idea to ask whether your salesperson is licensed by the state. This keeps them on their toes, in any event!

**referral program:** A program that many resorts offer that remunerates you if you provide referrals (names of potential buyers) who may want to purchase a similar product. Be wary of any resort that promises you a cash payment for these referrals, because this may be illegal.

**rescission period:** The legal period of time that you have to cancel the ownership after signing papers and get all your money back. These periods vary from no days to ten days depending on local laws. It's also referred to as the *cooling-off period.*

**Resort Condominiums International (RCI):** One of the two major exchange companies. *See also* **Interval International (II).**

**right to use:** A license or contractual membership right of occupancy in a timeshare or other common interest subdivision that's not coupled with an estate in real property. This is not the same as a deed, which in most cases is in effect until sold.

**season:** The time of year that the owner has a right to use his or her week. Seasons often determine the

price of the unit and the availability or flexibility in trading or exchanging the unit. Seasons generally reflect the demand at that resort.

**simple interest no prepayment penalty:** Although the interest rate charged by the seller may be very high, the seller may allow you to pay more than your monthly payment, thus reducing the length of the loan and the effective interest rate (although not the interest rate on the loan). Be sure to ask for details and be sure that these details are outlined on any financing papers you sign. *See also* **financing terms.**

**special assessments:** The amount of money that the owner is charged to cover items that are not covered by regular maintenance fees. Typically, resorts with ownership or membership on golf courses and waterfront assess special assessments. Be certain to ask about the history of assessment fees at your property and whether you have a vote in the issuance of these assessments.

**special warranty deed:** Includes a warranty of title and an agreement to defend claims against title arising during the company's ownership of the property. With this type of deed, you're protected by title insurance from the time the timeshare is first purchased.

**taxes:** The amount of money the owner will be charged every year to pay for property taxes. This money *may* be tax deductible.

**trading power:** The value of a timeshare week in regard to trading or exchanging for another week, whether at the same resort or at another resort.

**unit:** The specific room in a specific building (for example, unit 105, building 3, which is a one-bedroom unit that sleeps four people) that you purchase and is recorded on your deed. Although you may have purchased a floating week, there must be an actual unit assigned to your purchase to prevent overselling. *See also* **floating week.**

**week:** The week or weeks that you purchase which will be recorded on your deed. Although you may have purchased a floating week, there must be an actual week assigned to your purchase to prevent overselling. *See also* **fixed week, floating week.**

# Appendix C

# Timeshare Around the World

● ● ● ● ● ● ● ● ● ● ● ● ● ● ● ● ● ● ● ● ● ● ● ● ● ● ● ● ● ● ● ● ● ● ● ● ● ● ● ●

*C*urrently, Resort Condominiums International (RCI) has 4,000 resorts around the world. See Table C-1 for RCI's list of resort locations.

| Table C-1 | RCI Resort Locations |
|---|---|
| *Area/Country* | *Number of RCI Locations* |
| United States | 1,212 |
| Canada | 98 |
| Mexico | 258 |
| Bermuda, Bahamas, and the Caribbean | 193 |
| Central and South America | 316 |
| Europe | 995 |
| Africa and the Middle East | 265 |
| Asia/Pacific | 334 |
| Australia and New Zealand | 114 |

Currently, Interval International (II) has roughly 2,000 resorts worldwide. See Table C-2 for its locations.

| Table C-2 | II Resort Locations |
|---|---|
| *Area/Country* | *Number of II Locations* |
| United States | 906 |
| Canada | 37 |

*(continued)*

## Timeshare Around the World

## Table C-2 *(continued)*

| Area/Country | Number of II Locations |
| --- | --- |
| Caribbean and Atlantic Islands | 124 |
| Mexico and Central America | 80 |
| South America | 96 |
| Europe | 375 |
| Africa and the Middle East | 38 |
| Asia | 32 |
| Australia, New Zealand, and the South Pacific | 56 |

# Index

**• D •**

**• S •**

# Notes

# Notes

## BUSINESS, CAREERS & PERSONAL FINANCE

*Grant Writing For Dummies*
0-7645-5307-0

*Home Buying For Dummies*
0-7645-5331-3 *†

**Also available:**

- Accounting For Dummies †
  0-7645-5314-3
- Business Plans Kit For Dummies †
  0-7645-5365-8
- Cover Letters For Dummies
  0-7645-5224-4
- Frugal Living For Dummies
  0-7645-5403-4
- Leadership For Dummies
  0-7645-5176-0
- Managing For Dummies
  0-7645-1771-6

- Marketing For Dummies
  0-7645-5600-2
- Personal Finance For Dummies *
  0-7645-2590-5
- Project Management
  For Dummies
  0-7645-5283-X
- Resumes For Dummies †
  0-7645-5471-9
- Selling For Dummies
  0-7645-5363-1
- Small Business Kit For Dummies *†
  0-7645-5093-4

## HOME & BUSINESS COMPUTER BASICS

*Windows XP For Dummies*
0-7645-4074-2

*Excel 2003 For Dummies*
0-7645-3758-X

**Also available:**

- ACT! 6 For Dummies
  0-7645-2645-6
- iLife '04 All-in-One Desk Reference
  For Dummies
  0-7645-7347-0
- iPAQ For Dummies
  0-7645-6769-1
- Mac OS X Panther Timesaving
  Techniques For Dummies
  0-7645-5812-9
- Macs For Dummies
  0-7645-5656-8
- Microsoft Money 2004 For Dummies
  0-7645-4195-1

- Office 2003 All-in-One Desk
  Reference For Dummies
  0-7645-3883-7
- Outlook 2003 For Dummies
  0-7645-3759-8
- PCs For Dummies
  0-7645-4074-2
- TiVo For Dummies
  0-7645-6923-6
- Upgrading and Fixing PCs
  For Dummies
  0-7645-1665-5
- Windows XP Timesaving
  Techniques For Dummies
  0-7645-3748-2

## FOOD, HOME, GARDEN, HOBBIES, MUSIC & PETS

*Feng Shui For Dummies*
0-7645-5295-3

*Poker For Dummies*
0-7645-5232-5

**Also available:**

- Bass Guitar For Dummies
  0-7645-2487-9
- Diabetes Cookbook For Dummies
  0-7645-5230-9
- Gardening For Dummies *
  0-7645-5130-2
- Guitar For Dummies
  0-7645-5106-X
- Holiday Decorating For Dummies
  0-7645-2570-0
- Home Improvement All-in-One
  For Dummies
  0-7645-5680-0

- Knitting For Dummies
  0-7645-5395-X
- Piano For Dummies
  0-7645-5105-1
- Puppies For Dummies
  0-7645-5255-4
- Scrapbooking For Dummies
  0-7645-7208-3
- Senior Dogs For Dummies
  0-7645-5818-8
- Singing For Dummies
  0-7645-2475-5
- 30-Minute Meals For Dummies
  0-7645-2589-1

## INTERNET & DIGITAL MEDIA

*Digital Photography For Dummies*
0-7645-1664-7

*Starting an eBay Business For Dummies*
0-7645-6924-4

**Also available:**

- 2005 Online Shopping Directory
  For Dummies
  0-7645-7495-7
- CD & DVD Recording For Dummies
  0-7645-5956-7
- eBay For Dummies
  0-7645-5654-1
- Fighting Spam For Dummies
  0-7645-5965-6
- Genealogy Online For Dummies
  0-7645-5964-8
- Google For Dummies
  0-7645-4420-9

- Home Recording For Musicians
  For Dummies
  0-7645-1634-5
- The Internet For Dummies
  0-7645-4173-0
- iPod & iTunes For Dummies
  0-7645-7772-7
- Preventing Identity Theft
  For Dummies
  0-7645-7336-5
- Pro Tools All-in-One Desk
  Reference For Dummies
  0-7645-5714-9
- Roxio Easy Media Creator
  For Dummies
  0-7645-7131-1

**Separate Canadian edition also available**
**Separate U.K. edition also available**

Available wherever books are sold. For more information or to order direct: U.S. customers
visit www.dummies.com or call 1-877-762-2974.
U.K. customers visit www.wileyeurope.com or call 0800 243407. Canadian customers visit
www.wiley.ca or call 1-800-567-4797.

## SPORTS, FITNESS, PARENTING, RELIGION & SPIRITUALITY

0-7645-5146-9

0-7645-5418-2

**Also available:**

- Adoption For Dummies
  0-7645-5488-3
- Basketball For Dummies
  0-7645-5248-1
- The Bible For Dummies
  0-7645-5296-1
- Buddhism For Dummies
  0-7645-5359-3
- Catholicism For Dummies
  0-7645-5391-7
- Hockey For Dummies
  0-7645-5228-7

- Judaism For Dummies
  0-7645-5299-6
- Martial Arts For Dummies
  0-7645-5358-5
- Pilates For Dummies
  0-7645-5397-6
- Religion For Dummies
  0-7645-5264-3
- Teaching Kids to Read
  For Dummies
  0-7645-4043-2
- Weight Training For Dummies
  0-7645-5168-X
- Yoga For Dummies
  0-7645-5117-5

## TRAVEL

0-7645-5438-7

0-7645-5453-0

**Also available:**

- Alaska For Dummies
  0-7645-1761-9
- Arizona For Dummies
  0-7645-6938-4
- Cancún and the Yucatán
  For Dummies
  0-7645-2437-2
- Cruise Vacations For Dummies
  0-7645-6941-4
- Europe For Dummies
  0-7645-5456-5
- Ireland For Dummies
  0-7645-5455-7

- Las Vegas For Dummies
  0-7645-5448-4
- London For Dummies
  0-7645-4277-X
- New York City For Dummies
  0-7645-6945-7
- Paris For Dummies
  0-7645-5494-8
- RV Vacations For Dummies
  0-7645-5443-3
- Walt Disney World & Orlando
  For Dummies
  0-7645-6943-0

## GRAPHICS, DESIGN & WEB DEVELOPMENT

0-7645-4345-8

0-7645-5589-8

**Also available:**

- Adobe Acrobat 6 PDF
  For Dummies
  0-7645-3760-1
- Building a Web Site For Dummies
  0-7645-7144-3
- Dreamweaver MX 2004
  For Dummies
  0-7645-4342-3
- FrontPage 2003 For Dummies
  0-7645-3882-9
- HTML 4 For Dummies
  0-7645-1995-6
- Illustrator CS For Dummies
  0-7645-4084-X

- Macromedia Flash MX 2004
  For Dummies
  0-7645-4358-X
- Photoshop 7 All-in-One Desk
  Reference For Dummies
  0-7645-1667-1
- Photoshop CS Timesaving
  Techniques For Dummies
  0-7645-6782-9
- PHP 5 For Dummies
  0-7645-4166-8
- PowerPoint 2003 For Dummies
  0-7645-3908-6
- QuarkXPress 6 For Dummies
  0-7645-2593-X

## NETWORKING, SECURITY, PROGRAMMING & DATABASES

0-7645-6852-3

0-7645-5784-X

**Also available:**

- A+ Certification For Dummies
  0-7645-4187-0
- Access 2003 All-in-One Desk
  Reference For Dummies
  0-7645-3988-4
- Beginning Programming
  For Dummies
  0-7645-4997-9
- C For Dummies
  0-7645-7068-4
- Firewalls For Dummies
  0-7645-4048-3
- Home Networking For Dummies
  0-7645-42796

- Network Security For Dummies
  0-7645-1679-5
- Networking For Dummies
  0-7645-1677-9
- TCP/IP For Dummies
  0-7645-1760-0
- VBA For Dummies
  0-7645-3989-2
- Wireless All In-One Desk Reference
  For Dummies
  0-7645-7496-5
- Wireless Home Networking
  For Dummies
  0-7645-3910-8

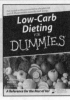